Barbara Woodhouse

The

NO BAD DOGS

Woodhouse Way

Grateful acknowledgment is made to the following for their photographs: On pp. 2, 15, 27: Peter Riding; pp. 10-11, 19: © Nicholas A. Spurling; pp. 32, 64, 101-105; Paul Chave; p. 36: Sunday Mirror; pp. 47, 120: Sun photographic Bureau, Ltd.; p. 50: Sally Fear; p. 51: John Drysdale; p. 79: Fox Photos, Ltd.; p. 127; BBC Copyright Photograph.

FIRESIDE
Simon & Schuster Building
Rockefeller Center
1230 Avenue of the Americas
New York, New York 10020

Published by Summit Books
First Fireside Edition 1992

Published by arrangement with George Rainbird Ltd, England

Designed by Eve Metz

Manufactured in the United States of America

20 19 18 17 16 15 14 13
20 19 18 17 Pbk.

First American Paperback Edition
Library of Congress Cataloging in Publication Data
Woodhouse, Barbara, date.
No Bad Dogs.
1. Dogs—Training. 2. Dogs—Behavior. I Title.
SF431.W73 1982 636.7'0887 81-21530
AACR2

ISBN 0-671-44962-1
ISBN 0-671-54185-4 Pbk.

Contents

Foreword

A LOT OF RUBBISH has been spoken about the psychoanalyzing of dogs in the modern world, and having now trained over 17,000 dogs in twenty years, I feel I am qualified to express an opinion on the subject of dog behavior.

For years I have been collecting data for this book from letters I have had from desperate or depressed dog owners whose dogs are causing them worry or despair. I feel I must help them further by debunking many ideas about dogs and their minds. Then at least the dogs' lives may be made more normal and their owners happy.

If dog owners recognize their dog's failure and their own personal problems, this is a hopeful sign. For many people realize only too well that even though they have owned perfect dogs in the past, today's vintage may not be the same. Their old theories and methods may be completely out of date.

With vast experience behind me I believe that unless a dog is unapproachably savage or mentally unsound, it can be made a decent member of society and a joy to own. Thus was coined my school motto, which is "There is no such thing as a difficult dog, only an inexperienced owner."

I sincerely hope this book will open the eyes of many to their dog's nature, help those in trouble and give hope to the despairing. Many will criticize what I say, but I have spared no one, least of all myself.

Overleaf: *A class awaits the next instruction.*

1 · My Casebook

MY CASEBOOK IS FULL of dog owners of every description. Oversentimental owners, owners in need themselves of immediate psychiatric help, owners who never should be owners, owners who have problems but who respond immediately to help given and whose lives are thereby changed for the better. There are owners who wish to imprint their ideas on me rather than letting me imprint my ideas on them, owners who come to me when tired of their dogs and wish me to agree that I think their dogs should be put to sleep, and get downright angry when I say the dog can easily be cured of what is wrong and I attempt to do so at once.

One lady drove up in a car and said her dog was impossible, fought every dog it met and would do nothing right, and her husband would only have it put to sleep if I said it was untrainable. This was a bullterrier, a breed known for its aggressive attitude toward other dogs, but in this case there was absolutely nothing wrong with the dog at all. I mixed it with other dogs, freed it with other dogs, made it stay in the "down" position for a prolonged period with other dogs, and found it a highly intelligent, highly obedient and loving animal. I refused to comply with the lady's wish for me to write to her husband and say it was untrainable. This story had a happy ending. She took a course and learned to love the dog instead of finding it a bore, but not many cases have such happy endings.

The worst cases under the title of "phobias" are those who project their own faults in character makeup onto their dogs. One lady arrived with a tiny poodle and said the dog had a terrible fear of loud noises, hated water, which the owner said was "eerie," and would not get onto a bus or a car without terror in its heart. The moment the owner stepped out of the car with a subdued husband following in the background I knew where the fault lay.

I put a choke chain on the dog and walked it down the road to a site where building was going on and huge brick trucks were tipping their loads with a tremendous noise every few minutes. The dog's tail was up, she was sniffing all the exciting country scents in a typical untroubled doggy manner, and the falling bricks and huffs and puffs of compressors, etc., had not the slightest effect on her. The next thing I did was to put dog and owners into my car and drive to a huge lake near us with "still water," which was supposed to be so "eerie" that the dog would be terrified. I let the dog off the lead and raced around with it, throwing sticks for it to retrieve, and then said, "Patty, go into the water and have a drink," which she promptly did, and paddled quite happily until I called her out and told the owner that as far as Patty was concerned there were no phobias in her life; all were in the lady's imagination and she was trying to project her own phobias about noise and eerie water into the dog's mind. On returning to my home the lady remarked to my husband, who is a doctor, that I had said *she* was the nut case. I hoped I had shown her who was to blame. I pointed out that with the proper choke chain, a few good jerks should the dog do anything wrong, and possibly a paddle in the lake with the dog by her, there would be no problem with the dog. All the dog needed was healthful open-air walks, a happy outlook on the owner's part and no ideas that the dog suffered any abnormality of temperament. Two days later my choke chain came back in the mail, so I supposed that anything I had done was to be completely disregarded. I had an idea that the root of the trouble in this case was marital, not animal.

Recently a man with a golden retriever drove a long way to see me. He said the dog refused to come out of the car and pulled terribly to get back into it if ejected forcibly. The dog was terrifically fat, which made the handling of it an almost impossible feat, really needing a strong man to achieve the jerks that the dog should have on the choke chain to put sense into it. The retriever had a short lead, a wrong thin-linked choke chain which would have hurt the dog had it been closed on the neck, and the owner's attitude on arriving at my place was "I know you can't cure this."

The first thing I did was put my own thick-linked choke chain on the dog and a strong four-foot lead, open the door of the station wagon and call the dog by name, with a commanding voice and a very welcoming voice alternating. The dog just stayed lying down trembling in the car, so I got tough. I said, "Randy, come" and when I gave a very sharp downward jerk on his choke chain the dog bounced out in one leap; then I praised him and let him get back in the car. The shivering started again; I repeated this sequence three times and then took the dog for a walk. As he pulled so terribly on the lead, walks for this dog had, I was told, been impossible. The only freedom he had ever got was when his owners could get him out of the car in some safe place and let him run about, after which he would immediately head back for the car and stay shivering outside.

The jerks on the choke chain did the trick. The dog's tail rose from between its legs, he stopped pulling on the lead and when we eventually returned to the car, I opened the back and the dog jumped in and lay down. I gave the command "Randy, come," and the dog leaped out, anticipating another fun walk, which he got. After that there was never any trouble about shivering or not wanting to get out of the car. I suggested the dog be put on a diet immediately to make the effort of going for a nice long walk less tiring exercise for Randy and less risk to his heart as he was three years old.

The phobias I meet are very often connected with the show ring. Dogs that won't be handled by judges, men or women, and who all would be champions according to their owners if only they would stand still for examination—not bite the judge, or stay put on a table, or keep their tails up while being looked at, or sit in the ring. This may sound like a tall order to accomplish; yet in fact it all starts with the same routine obedience.

One can train dogs up to almost human standards and teach them to reason things out, which many people say is impossible. I have proved with my own dogs many a time that dogs reason if the owners make an effort to develop their brains from the moment the dogs come into the house. I am appalled at the number of dogs whose eyes show little intelligence, whose knowledge of the meaning of words and thoughts is strangely lacking, and whose main idea is either copulation or hunting, the owner being useful only for providing the essentials of life and a home to guard. It is sad how much these owners have missed in companionship and in understanding their dog. But of course to train a dog to a high standard of intelligence as well as obedience takes almost as much time and understanding as teaching a five-year-old child the three R's. Many owners are far too unimaginative in their characters ever to achieve this standard of intelligence in their dogs. They may be too sentimental; they may abandon training too quickly with the idea that their dog doesn't like training. Dogs like training if the owners make it exciting enough. The best owners are outgoing, full of fun, yet gentle and loving as well as firm, and if necessary can appear angry if the dog transgresses.

2·Nervous Dogs

WHEN I GET A NERVOUS DOG that won't be handled by strangers or a judge, the first thing I do is to put a choke chain on it. This very often has a devastating effect on the owner, who immediately has visions of all her precious Afghan's hair being rubbed off, or his Samoyed's hair turning black where the choke chain meets the neck. It takes me a long time to convince owners that if the choke chain never closes on the neck, which is my method, how can it damage hair? The dog that won't allow a judge to handle it must have a thick-linked choke chain on even if it is a one-and-a-half-pound Chihuahua. Sentimental talk about the chain being too heavy carries no weight with me; the chains weigh only two and a half ounces, and even a Chihuahua can carry that load without too much discomfort. I consider the thin show leads with which dogs are practically strung up far more uncomfortable for the dogs. In my opinion the idea that the correct choke chain is cruel and that dogs don't like them is nonsense. I can understand the wrong type being unkind, like the spiked collars or the very thin linked ones. Very large linked ones are quite harmless; in my opinion most choke chains are used incorrectly. I teach my owners to throw their hands forward, jerk sharply downward and immediately let go with the left hand, still keeping the right hand on the lead. In fact, I have everyone repeat, "Throw the hands forward, jerk and let go" together before we start using the choke chain.

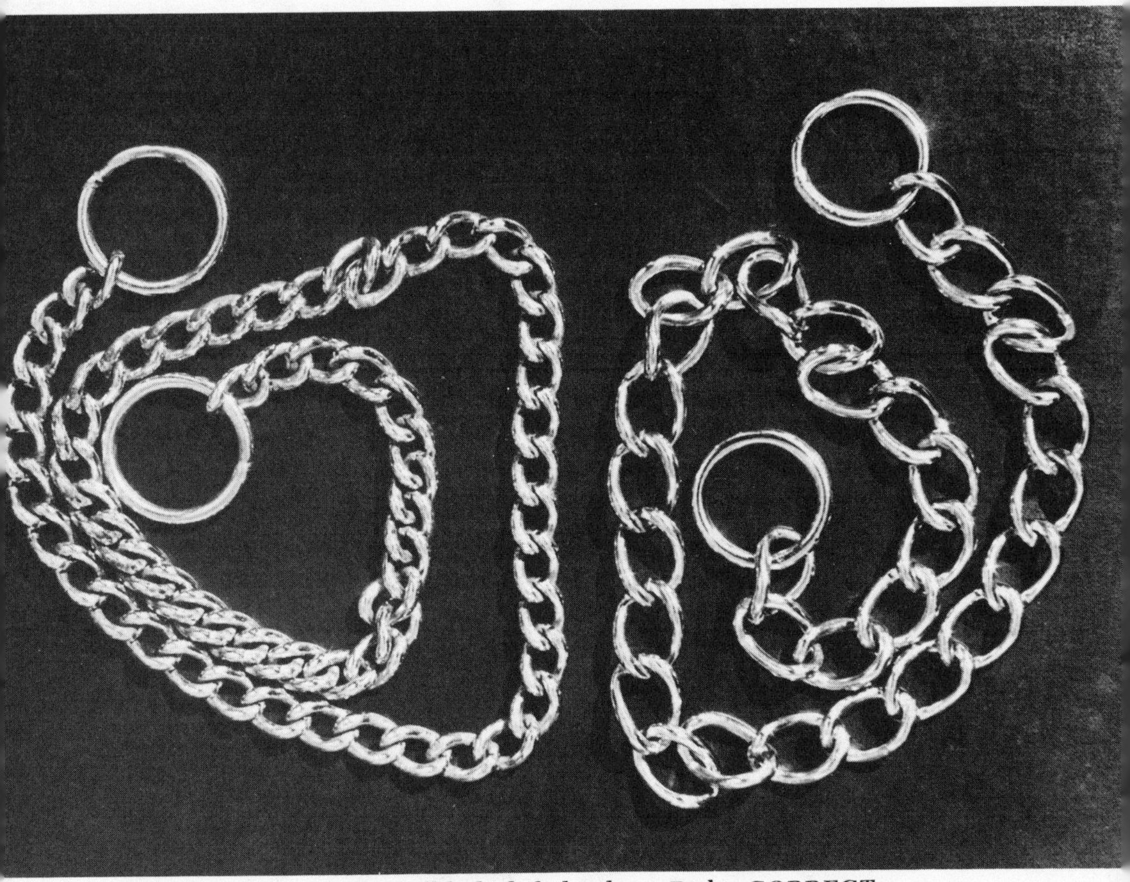

Left: *WRONG. Cruel, small-linked choke chain.* Right: *CORRECT. Large-linked choke chain won't hurt the dog.*

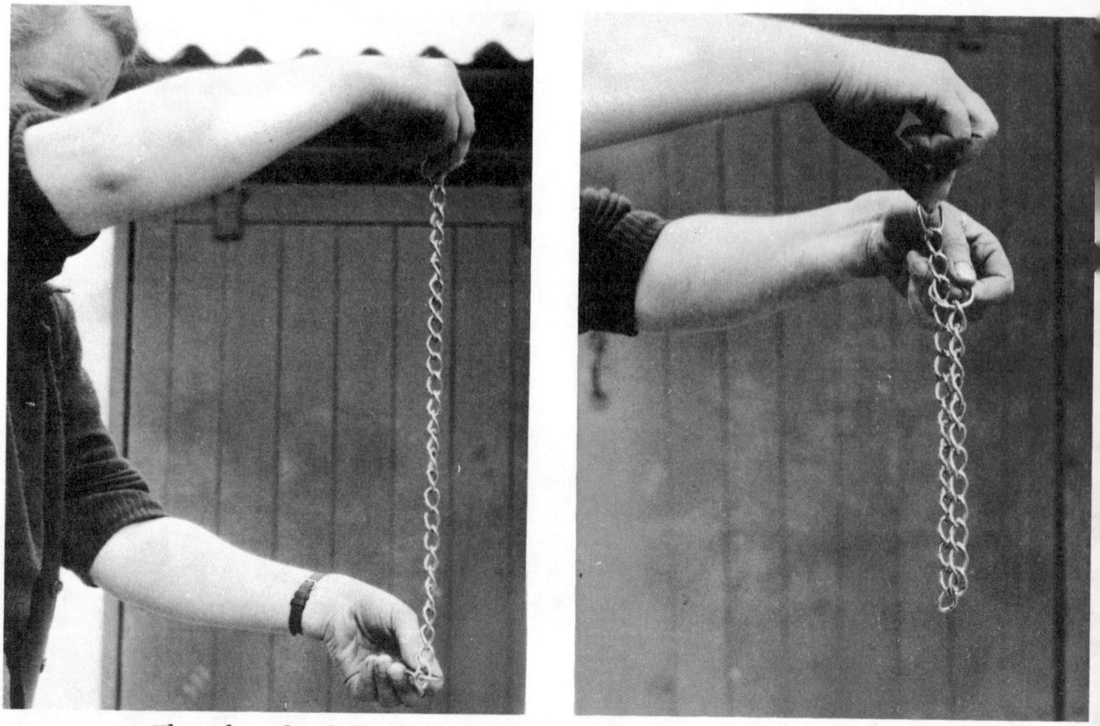

Threading the choke chain.

Unless the hands are thrown forward you don't get the lead loose enough to allow the quick jerk. The dogs should not even see the jerk, it should be so quick.

The next excuse I get from nervous or unbelieving owners is that they haven't the strength to jerk a big dog. I point out that strength is not needed. I myself have an injured spine after a car accident; yet I can jerk a large Saint Bernard and get the same result that I get with a tiny papillon or Yorkie. It is a knack that is vital to learn. Sometimes I put the choke chain on my own wrist and act as the dog for the owner to practice on so that the poor dog should not suffer the incorrect jerks the owner gives until she has been really indoctrinated with the correct quick action.

Let us take the cases of nervous dogs that won't allow a judge or stranger to approach them and open their mouths for examination. My first instruction is for the owner to learn the correct tone of voice and the command "Talk," for it will be on this word "Talk" that the whole training is based. This, the dog must, if necessary, learn the hard way. If when the owner points to the person the dog is to allow to handle him, he backs away, he is jerked back into position, given a most loving tickle on the ribs at the side of the body, which is kept up throughout the initial training, and again jerked back into position if he backs away. He soon gets tired of being jerked back and resignedly stands. Then he gets enormous praise in a fairly high pitched voice which is opposite to the low commanding tones of the order "Talk."

Left: *WRONG way. Choke chain will not release if put on upside-down.*
Right: *CORRECT way. Choke chain will free itself like this when released.*

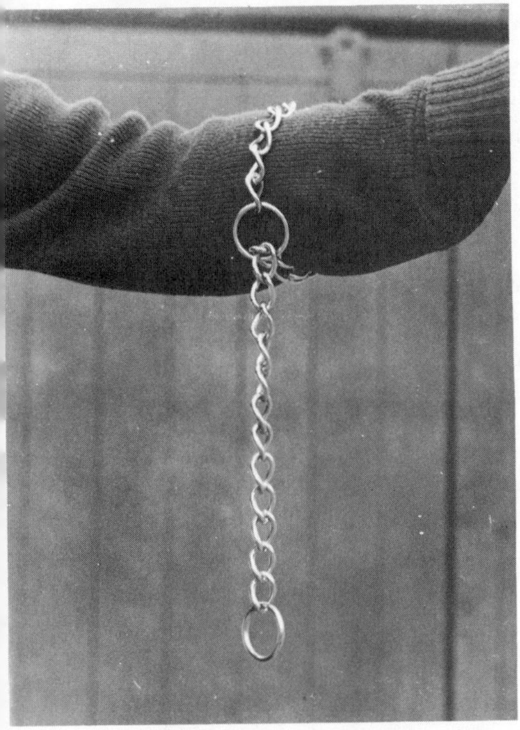

It is quite essential for the owner to stand away from the dog. No show dog is allowed to be strung up on its leash; they have to stay standing on the command "Wait," then be placed. The owner has a loose lead and stands at least eighteen inches away from the dog. I loathe to see exhibitors forever placing their dogs. Place them, leave them and relax. If you train a dog to do this stand every day for a few minutes—it will soon learn. I believe it is quite possible to achieve this behavior in a few minutes with the right confidence on the part of the trainer. People who come here with phobias that their dogs will not like judges need to cast that idea out of their minds and believe that the dogs will do as they are told.

Tickling tummies slowly and gently works wonders. Never use a rubbing motion; this makes dogs bad-tempered. A gentle tickle with the tips of the fingers is all that is necessary to induce calm in a dog. I hate strangers who go up to dogs with their hands held to the dog's nose, usually palm toward themselves. How does the dog know that the hand doesn't hold something horrid? The palm should always be shown to the dog and should go straight down to between the dog's front legs and tickle gently with a soothing voice to accompany the action. Very often the dog raises its back leg in a scratching movement, it gets so much pleasure from this.

The person acting as the judge in the training session must walk around the dog, appraising it from all angles. Then the owner gives the command "Talk" and points toward the "judge" with an upward swing of the finger. This usually raises the dog's head, which improves the general silhouette. The "judge" should then approach the dog. If the dog sits back, give the lead to the person doing the supposed judging and make him step back quickly, giving quite sharp but small jerks on the lead with the word "Come." The dog may resist; if it does, it is essential to continue this backward

Even a very small dog can wear the correct choke chain.

movement, often changing direction until the dog realizes he has got to cooperate. Then the "judge" handles the dog's head, scratches its chest and examines its teeth. Very seldom does the dog object to this after these instructions are carried out. If more owners would hand the lead to their friends and helpers when the dog refuses to be handled, the trouble would be solved very quickly. I have often cured a nervous dog in less than thirty minutes by this firm compulsion method.

Hold the lead with the right hand, keeping the left hand free to jerk if necessary.

3 · Dogs with Phobias

ONE PHOBIA I HAVE OFTEN SEEN is that of small dogs who won't go near another dog. The owners are usually shy themselves and the dogs are only mirroring the owners' lack of really wishing to be gregarious. The best way to teach this type of dog to ignore other dogs but to walk with them and past them without leaping away is to use two dogs. Put both on choke chains and just jerk them forward with small leaps at a very fast pace. They can't do otherwise than go together if this is done. Then drop the leads, give a thunderous command "Wait," and the dogs are usually so surprised at the tone of voice and backward hand signal over their heads that they stand quite still for a few seconds. With repeat performances of this, the dogs ignore each other and other dogs and are on the road to a cure.

Recently I had a long phone call from a lady whose dog refused to get on buses and trains. After intimating that she just picked it up and took it on these vehicles, she said it would become completely hysterical if this was done. I began to get suspicious and asked her if she was herself an agoraphobic, and she admitted she was. It was her terror at leaving the shelter of her home that made the dog do what it did. There is no cure for the dog in this case, for

A class learns to ignore other dogs and await the masters' next command.

it never does anything wrong with a normal handler. Dozens of times in my life I have taken dogs happily where the owners say they won't go. I've stood in the middle of a busy road on a traffic island with a dog that is supposed to be frightened of traffic and seen no fear whatsoever, ridden in cars with so-called carsick dogs and found no car sickness at all, providing the dog was resting in the down position with its head on my lap and a gentle tickle given to its tummy.

Recently a lady with a Labrador said that her dog wouldn't be brushed, that the sight of the brush made it hysterical. I think the reason the dog apparently didn't like being brushed was that the brush was far too hard and the dog had a delicate skin. I made it lie down on its side and progressed from tickling its tummy with my hand to smoothing the dog's side with the wrong side of the brush. The dog went to sleep. Then I changed the brush over to its bristle side, and from then on the dog never objected to being brushed. Again, confidence is necessary on the part of the person who is going to do the brushing.

A vice I've met with in quite a number of small dogs is that they bite any person who approaches too close to the owner. This is nearly always caused by the owner's hugging the dog to her chest. The quickest way to cure a dog of this habit is always to hold it with its quarters on your hip and your hand underneath its chest, with one finger through the front legs to support its front. It gets confidence by being held away from the owner's body and is then handed to several people willing to take it, suitably protected by gloves if necessary. I never use gloves, I prefer to allow the dog to snap at me if it must. I find that if you stay with your hand relaxed, the dog spits it out rather than bites it, but I know this is not easy for everyone to do. Talking about gloves, I had a curious case one day of a lady who arrived in very smart town clothes—complete with cotton gloves—to train her dog. She would not take the gloves off. I tried to convince her that human contact is the most important asset in training a dog and getting its confidence. (As much as possible, I lay my face against my pupils' muzzles and give them a kiss behind the ear, which is quite safe from the risk of infection.)

If you wear gloves, you don't get that human contact, and it is in a way similar to smacking a dog with a newspaper, something I strongly disapprove of. If a dog has to be smacked, use your hand; then it is you who are doing the scolding, not a newspaper.

I think the word "won't" is the word I hate most in dealing with dogs with phobias. In my opinion there is no such thing as "won't." There may be an initial "can't" in the early stages of training, but "won't" is made up by the owner to cover a multitude of excuses, none of which I tolerate. In my opinion, if the word "won't" is allowed to excuse bad behavior and nothing changes that attitude, the dog is not worth keeping, for the dog would be unhappy in the world of "won't" and the owner ineffective and unlikely to get much joy from the dog. It is for this reason I always take the dog away from the owner for a few minutes on first meeting it and show the owner it *will* do what is asked if the right tone of voice is used, the right happy attitude of mind cultivated, and above all the really happy praise given the dog when it does as is wanted.

In praising dogs I always use the words "What a good dog." I have lined a class of dogs up and told the owners to praise them in their usual manner, then told them to prefix the praise with the word "what." The effect on the dogs is undeniable. For some extraordinary reason the word "what" electrifies them and gives them so much more pleasure than ordinary praise. After telling listeners to a broadcast to say this to their dogs, I had dozens of letters saying it really does work.

4 • Tails Up

ONE OF THE MOST DIFFICULT problems I very often have to cope with is getting a depressed dog's tail up and making the dog happy not only in its ordinary life but for the show ring too. This, to many exhibitors, is completely defeating, and the depression the owner feels at seeing the dog's tail down between the legs is passed to the dog and so the trouble never ends.

Many dogs hate shows, and I think if a dog really hates every second of the show business, it will never win the highest honors whatever its beauty and conformation. For it is an outgoing, happy character that adds to the beauty of any show dog.

I think in the first place the dogs must be taught that this show business is not meant to be just fun. It is meant to be a lesson, and when it is over, fun will be the reward. That is why I hate "ring-craft" classes, for who is to teach ringcraft to a lot of breeds of dogs with different temperaments? Many depressed dogs have suffered from this type of training. I think it much better for the owner to go to several shows by herself and watch the experts at work, and then go home and practice for short spells at a time the same handling that appears to win the major prizes. Professional handlers so often win the top prizes because they instill confidence in a dog while its owners do not. Everyone wants so much to win that I think even the most hardened of exhibitors must feel nervous when showing their own dogs. The professional handler has supreme confidence and has trained the dog by his own technique to his required standard; yet I would much rather see an owner get to the top with his own efforts.

Tails drop into the misery stance between the legs for many reasons: the dog is unsure of the owner's wishes, the dog is bored, the dog is frightened, the dog is tired. All these conditions must be eliminated if the dog's tail is to assume its correct position.

Tails can be made to stay upright in the case of small dogs such as Pekes, Chihuahuas, papillons, and Poms, by brushing your hand with the lightest possible touch from the base of the tail to the tip in a very fast flick movement. This gives out static electricity, and the tail will stay up for the short time that the judge is looking at the dog. Eventually the dog so likes this flick movement that the tail will stay up. But the quickest way to start the tail coming from between the dog's legs is to run really fast, giving the quick jerks on the choke chain I have recommended before. The dog's tail is there to balance him, the jerks unbalance him and the tail rises to counteract the loss of balance. That is why I say, jerk the dog, a pull is useless. In time, as you get ready to run with the dog, he will be so used to being unbalanced by jerks that he will hold his tail up from the beginning in case the owner intends jerking. Dogs are very quick to learn. Incidentally, to stop a dog from sitting in the ring, loosely tie the ends of a soft lead around its tummy every time you stop and give the command "Stand." Should it attempt to sit, pull it into the standing position by this lead. This takes very few minutes to teach and is much better than use of the hand.

The best way to make a dog hold its tail in the correct manner is, of course, happiness, and this happiness stems only from the owner's treatment of the dog. Is it getting enough doggy pursuits? Does it look forward with happy anticipation to an outing with the owner, or is it just accustomed to a miserable walk around the block without the fun of ever being free to play and romp with other dogs? Is it taught lots of new things to do and given lots of praise on achieving these things, or is kennel life its existence with only routine exercise? A clever dog is seldom a depressed dog. Try bringing a show dog with tail trouble into your home and teaching

Tails come up when you move fast with the dog, giving quick jerks on the choke chain.

it things. Cultivate an interesting tone of voice. I taught my dogs police work, and when at shows, I only had to use the voice that meant we were going to have to chase after a criminal to make the ears alert and the dog's whole attitude one of excited expectancy. This was when the dog looked at its best. Its attention was on the direction I had initially pointed to, which, in training, means that the person to be caught had gone that way. I doubt if this would work with all small dogs, although I did use it with our toy terrier, who liked nothing better than a chase.

Nerves seem to be the most usual cause of tails between legs. Nerves can be cured in a very short time. When the dog is no longer afraid, it naturally holds its tail in the happy position. Sentimental owners will never cure nerves, for nerves can be cured only by confident owners.

5·Schizophrenia

INCREASINGLY DOGS ARE BITING their owners, dogs that have perhaps been faithful and contented companions for some time, and distraught owners phone me to know what to do. It is extremely difficult to help people over the phone, for I can't tell whether the cause is one of many things that make a dog suddenly revert to this type of retaliation. I am always suspicious that this is another case of schizophrenia. The usual symptoms are a complete lack of warmth in the eye, as if the dog had a headache; the lower lids often become red and the eyes have no depth to them. The insides of the ears also become red, as if the dog had a toxemia and a frightful headache. He may suddenly viciously bite the person he previously loved most, and then some minutes later be perfectly normal; the ears return on the inside to a pale color, and the eyes regain their depth and look again for love—and I am sure the dog does not remember biting at all.

I myself had forty-six stitches in one arm and sixteen in the other from a bulldog I'd been training. He did all the exercises to perfection and had been a very loving and lovable chap. I had him in a field on a lead, talking to his owner; the dog was behind me when suddenly I didn't know what had hit me. This animal leaped onto my right arm and bit right down to the tendons. A fraction of an inch more and that arm would have been crippled for life. I managed with superhuman effort to get his mouth open, and he got me on the left hand and bit that to the bone. Then he dropped off, wagged his tail and obviously expected the loving treatment he had had throughout his training. It was only then that the owner told me he had bitten her five times. The vet agreed with me that this was schizophrenia and put the dog to sleep. I feel sure many of these unprovoked attacks that kill children or do some terrible damage to other human beings are cases of schizophrenia. I once told the owner of a Labrador to put his dog to sleep when he described unprovoked aggression in the dog, and he said his wife would be heartbroken if he did that and he was going to give it another chance. Ten days later the dog bit his small child, who was terribly injured in the face. The dog was put away. I often wonder why people phone me and don't take my advice. I have no axe to grind in saying put the dog to sleep, if I really feel the dog is not safe. My first idea always is to try to train the dog. My only other method of saving the dog's life is sending it to a vet to have all its teeth out. One dog who bit a child four times had this done on my advice and is now eleven years old; even if it made an attack it could do no damage.

Nobody knows the cause of schizophrenia. Many people say it is a hormone upset, many others think it is a dietetic upset; but until the veterinary profession finds some definite clues to its cause, whether hereditary or formed in the lifetime, no one with a dog that behaves as I described should keep it unless it is muzzled, or with no teeth, for these dogs only have to get someone in an artery for that person perhaps to die before help could be obtained. I am very shocked at the deterioration in dogs' temperament these days. At shows, dogs should be disqualified at the slightest sign of bad temperament, but this does not happen. I've seen a bad-tempered Doberman win a challenge certificate. I've seen a very nervous Irish wolfhound that would not stand up properly be placed over a beautiful dog with a wonderful temperament. I am not a show person, so don't know what possible excuse the judge could have had for rating the dogs like this, but I think the judge should not be a judge and encourage the breeding of nervous or bad-tempered dogs. Very often the two run side by side.

6 · *Jumping Up*

MANY PEOPLE COMPLAIN THAT their dogs jump up, tear their clothes in so doing and are a menace to visitors, old people and children. What they don't seem to understand is that this jumping up is really a compliment. The dog only wishes to be near the face of its owner, which is a dog's way of showing affection. This of course differs from the jumping up and biting which some dogs do. I remember a Pyrenean mountain dog (Great Pyrenees) who arrived with a tiny middle-aged lady and proceeded to pin her against the wall and go straight for her throat. I grabbed it from her, and it tried to do the same thing to me. I had the worst few minutes of my life with this animal; it really meant to kill me, I think. However, by tightening my hold on its choke chain I got the desired effect, and it flopped to the ground beaten and winded. After that I kissed it and stroked it, and that dog became the gentlest animal imaginable. (I have a lovely picture of it with its head on my shoulder.) All this goes to show that the terrible "leader of the pack" instinct still exists in the world of dogs and can come to the fore if not curbed when the dog is at an early age.

Dogs must be mastered at some time in their lives if respect is to be gained in the master-dog relationship. When this confrontation takes place (if it takes place) varies from dog to dog, but the dog must never be the winner. Bones are very often "the bone of contention" and can lead to dangerous encounters. Unless a dog is

For jumping up, the correction is to teach dog to sit and stay on command.

taught in its early days to give up whatever is in its mouth, on command, confrontations may occur. The most dangerous side of this bone business is that a dog may get too near some small child when it has its bone and could attack the child in the mistaken idea that the child wanted to take the bone. I don't believe in bones for dogs after the age of about three months. They are not necessary, and veterinarians say they can be positively harmful. It is much better to keep the teeth clean by having the tartar scraped off.

If the dog jumps up in a nice, friendly manner, the correction is to teach the dog to sit on command and stay sitting. Then as it approaches it is given the command "Sit" in plenty of time for it to drop into that position. Then the owner should of course get down on her knees and love the dog. At that height the dog can be near the owner's face and get loving hands to gently scratch its chest.

To break a dog of the habit of jumping up takes two people, its owner and a helper. The owner comes into the house or yard where the dog is on a long cord and a correct choke chain. The owner should have been out for some time if possible so that the dog will be especially pleased to see her. The other helper holds the cord. As the owner approaches the dog the long cord should be quite loose and as the dog goes to jump up, the cord should be jerked really hard by the helper until the dog is pulled very sharply and unexpectedly to the ground with the command "Down." If this is done several times, the dog has no idea where this correction is coming from and thinks well before repeating his jumping up. It usually takes about a quarter of an hour at odd times to teach a dog this lesson, *but* the dog should not be depressed by this treatment; it must get enormous praise when it doesn't jump up, especially if it sits in front of the owner, waiting for the praise it so deserves.

7 · Licking

LICKING THE FACE OF ANYONE by a dog should be firmly stopped. I know a dog caresses by licking; it is its way of showing love and appreciation of the person it does it to. But if it is stopped from doing this as a small puppy, it learns to lay its face against the owner's cheek without the licking. Licking, after all, can be a cause of infection to owners in rare cases, and not all dogs live a completely clean life. They eat manure, or lick their behinds—not only their own but those of other dogs who might not be so healthy as yours. Therefore I train all my dogs on the command "No lick" to be kissed by me behind their ears and to have their chests very slowly and gently scratched. So many people rub their dogs when praising them, and this I know for certain makes dogs bad-tempered. At a class once I saw a boy rubbing his dog when I gave the command, at the end of the exercise they were doing, "Praise your dog." I went up to him and rubbed his hair and asked him how he liked it. He went very red in the face and said he didn't like it at all—in fact, he felt like "bashing me one." Well, if he felt like "bashing me one," what did his dog feel like? Yet if his dog did anything like growling or biting, it would be severely reprimanded for no fault of its own. Rubbing the hair the wrong way is particularly obnoxious to a dog, whereas the gentle smoothing of the hair on the chest or on the rump is particularly pleasing to the dog. They love being scratched on top of the tail; it is an area of pleasure. There are many areas of pleasure, behind the ears, under the lower jaw, on the ribs behind the front legs, on the tummy and especially between the front legs. Owners must find out which pleases each individual dog best and keep that pleasure for a reward, as well as to please the dog.

Excessive licking of their bodies by dogs may indicate an allergy, constipation or a skin disease. People sometimes imagine that dogs wash themselves like cats; well, they don't. Sometimes when they get their paws wet, you will see dogs licking them to dry them, just as a female dog licks her puppies to clean and dry them.

Dogs should be allowed to lick one's hand—hands can easily be washed before touching food—but, generally, licking should be avoided and stopped at an early age.

8 · Dirty Dogs

MY "IN" TRAY IS FULL of letters from owners of dirty dogs—dogs that are taken out for exercise and then return to the house and at once go to their favorite spot in the home and relieve themselves. The damage to carpets can be enormous as, unless one immediately neutralizes the urine with some commercial fluid for the purpose, the carpet not only smells but eventually loses its color, especially if the animal soiling it is a bitch. Not only that, the smell is the signal for the dog to relieve itself again and again on the same spot. The owner may think that by washing the place the dog has fouled with detergents or disinfectants, she has removed the scent for the dog, but in fact she hasn't. Therefore it is useless scolding the dog; it is only doing what nature prompted, using only one chosen place for its toilet.

The cure is simple providing there is nothing physically wrong with the dog: change the site. This can be done by confining the dog to an indoor kennel for about three days, so that it is either carried or rushed out from the kennel to the spot the owner has chosen for its toilet. Otherwise, take the dog away from home for a few days. It is most unlikely it will soil in a new home at first and can then easily be trained to relieve itself on command. Once this is learned, housebreaking is easy. Many bitches won't relieve themselves away from home and their accustomed places anyway and will retain their urine until nearly bursting. This is the proof that this change of environment does the trick. They must not of course be free in anyone's home until they have adopted a place out of doors for their functions. The most important thing of all is to praise the dog generously when eventually it does do right outside. It is amazing how quickly a dog picks up the happy praising tone of voice when he does perform on command. I have often had ten-week-old puppies completely clean and performing all they ought to on my command. One eight-week-old Dalmatian, star of a dog food commercial, I housebroke in two hours, and thenceforth he relieved himself on command wherever I told him to. When he was eventually sold to a very luxurious home at twelve weeks old he never made a mistake. His manners were impeccable.

When I advocate keeping a puppy in an indoor kennel for three days, I do not mean it cannot go out for play and exercise. What I mean is, do not let it free in the home until the association of ideas as to the place it may use for its functions has been clearly built up. This must be out of doors; that is why it is easiest to housebreak a puppy in summer. If, however, the weather is very bad the puppy can be free, say in the kitchen, after relieving itself outside, for about half an hour before being put back in its kennel. It is surprising how often a puppy can pass urine, and the owner must constantly watch it and pick it up and pop it out if it shows any signs of sniffing around. An adult dog must be taken outside for exercise and not allowed the freedom of the house at all for three days. If it doesn't relieve itself out of doors, put it back in its kennel and try again in an hour or so. Once you achieve what you wish outside you are on the way to a permanent cure.

By being confined in a kennel for three days the dog quickly enlarges the size of its bladder and achieves bladder control, which is so necessary in a puppy. No animal willingly soils its bed. The regularity and number of times the puppy or dog can be taken out of course governs the speed with which the animal will learn to be clean.

So many owners today go to work, leaving their dog at home alone for long periods. They leave newspapers for the dog's toilet, which I think a revolting idea. If they must have a dog under these unsuitable conditions, they must expect somewhat unstable behavior.

No one should leave a dog for more than three hours without taking it out. Small puppies could not last this time. I feel if owners have to inflict these conditions on a dog, it would be better to buy an older housebroken dog in the first place.

Given a good run before the owner goes to work, the puppy should be able to last out until lunchtime.

Another very trying misdemeanor owners write about in dogs, in females in particular, involves the involuntary passing of urine when excited or frightened. The answer to this is of course training the dog to lie down and stay down on command, so that the squatting and uncontrolled wetting does not occur. Remaining in the down for quite long periods teaches a dog calmness and control.

It is particularly essential to insist on the down when visitors are arriving, for it is at this time that dogs are particularly prone to disgrace themselves, especially if a visitor tries to talk to them. Training to lie down and stay down should start at an early age. A trained dog is one that trusts its owner and the outside world. It is usually calm under all circumstances, is seldom carsick, is seldom a fighter, and takes in its stride any upheaval in the home. This trust comes only with daily training, with firm insistence on immediate obedience and then much praise.

I think most of the mental upsets except schizophrenia are caused by owners. I think most puppies are born normal, but some are made abnormal by their upbringing. Too many people are oversentimental and unable to deliver clear, firm commands. They end up with dirty dogs, biting dogs, disobedient dogs for several reasons. They think the dogs will grow out of their faults; this seldom happens. They think biting puppies are only biting because they are teething; this is wrong. Puppies bite because they want to be master. In sensible circles we don't allow puppies to teethe or bite on our fingers; a firm command "No bite" puts an end to this. One other reason for lack of correction: such owner words as "Oh, he's so sweet." Sweet the puppy may be at ten weeks, but he may turn out to be a likely candidate for being put to sleep at twelve months if he is allowed to continue unchecked.

The owners' voices can also make many dogs delinquent: the hopelessly inadequate tone on giving a command, together with the lack of meaningful words, the dreadfully flat tone they use for praise and the laziness of their movements all go to make a dog bored and uncaring. For example, if the owner sees a puppy just about to soil the floor or actually in the act, she should leap to scold it and pick it up and put it out. That leap instills into the dog's mind that there is something wrong with what he was doing or was about to do. A loud "Naughty dog" completes the correction. Never rub a dog's nose in what it has done—that is useless and not understood by a dog, and it is unhygienic and unkind.

If a reasonably adult dog continues to have dirty habits, restrict its fluid intake after 4 P.M. and of course confine it in an indoor kennel. People often go on far too long giving their puppies milk. I think after six months old this is unnecessary and adds to the fluid intake because the puppy likes it; then it has to pass more urine. With correct feeding and adequate supplement of minerals and trace elements, the dog should not need milk.

9·Getting to Know Your Dog

I GET MASSES OF LETTERS from people who wish me to choose the breed or sort of dog they should have. They usually write me reams about what they don't want, instead of fully writing to me about their homes, their children, their relatives, their other animals, the amount of time they can give to their dog, etc. They may say they've heard all long-eared dogs get canker, that all dachshunds get follicular mange, and class all dogs of that and other particular breeds under one heading as "impossible."

Dogs are no different from human beings in the wide range of characteristics and temperaments they possess. Dogs can have nervous breakdowns, just as human beings can, but dogs get typed as bad-tempered or disobedient. Few people think of the stresses of modern life, the noise of traffic, the perpetual human ratrace which affects the dog as its owner is forever dashing out of the front door, leaving the dog behind bewildered. The slower-ordered life of the past has almost disappeared for dogs and owners, and some dogs are put to sleep for conduct that could easily be corrected if only their owners would understand them and give them time.

The first characteristic to understand about dogs is that to them any change of home is traumatic. I was watching a TV program recently on disturbed children, and the only apparent cause for their being disturbed was that their parents had split up and the children had been put in foster care. Has it ever struck a new dog owner that exactly this has happened to a dog and that it takes time to adjust to a new home, new rules, new food, new people? Seldom is this given much thought. The new owners conclude that they are acceptable to a dog, in spite of the fact that to a dog they may not have the right scent. They may not handle him correctly; their voices may grate; they may have someone in the house who hates dogs; they may have an enemy cat that would willingly scratch out the new dog's eyes if he isn't careful to avoid it.

People should understand life from a dog's point of view before blaming him for everything that goes wrong. Mothers-to-be buy every book they can on baby welfare, but hundreds of people buy dogs with very little knowledge of them and then blame the dog for behavior they don't approve of. I would suggest that before anyone gets a dog, he should examine his knowledge of the breed he is choosing. Talk to people who have owned these dogs; see them at a dog show. If the breed shows aggression toward other dogs in the ring, or extreme nervousness when handled by the judge, think twice before buying one. Temperament faults are the most difficult to cure, and it may be costly to have professional help.

Think about how much exercise you are going to be able to give your dog; if it is somewhat restricted due to either your age, your work or your health, don't buy a Great Dane or a Doberman. Think about the dog's coat; have you time to brush it as often as it needs? There is nothing more horrible than an Old English sheepdog or a bearded collie all matted.

Make up your mind what role the dog has to play in your home. Is it just a pet? If so, you can often buy a puppy not up to show standard cheaper from a breeder than one with show potential, but don't rave if you take it to the local show and find it has an undershot jaw or other fault, for you must have known it had some fault to be sold cheaper. Don't take it out on the dog, for dogs understand your moods and your thoughts, and if you are thinking unpleasant things about your dog, he will pick it up and be downhearted. You must be prepared to get to know what your dog is feeling and thinking, if you are to get the best out of him. Telepathic communication with one's dog is something everybody should try to achieve. I know few will reach this height of understanding, but it is worth striving for.

Try to understand when your dog perhaps doesn't feel 100 percent well and leave out the long walk or the training for that day. Usually the eye of a dog gives away his health and his mood. When I am training, my eyes are forever watching the eyes of the dog I am training. I then know whether he intends to cooperate or whether his mind is on other things. If his mind is elsewhere, I become much firmer with him until he realizes second best is not good enough for me or, in due course, for his owner. But the other side of the situation is the mind of the owner. Is he really concentrating on the dog's behavior or is his mind also wandering? If so, he should give up training for that day, as one should do if not feeling well or in a bad mood. Dogs are very sympathetic animals if truly loved. They seem to sense when quiet sympathy is what is wanted from them and do not intrude on the owner's thoughts or actions when the owner is not in the mood. But this takes understanding from the owner and a lot of companionship with the dog, as well as talking to the dog.

I wonder how many words in a day the average owner speaks to the dog. Usually it is very few. Among those few may be "Din-din," "Walkie," "Shut up," "Go to your bed," and "Good boy" or "Good girl," but actual conversation is not all that common. I used to really talk to my dogs, whose understanding became "almost human."

I hope people reading this book will gain an insight into their dog's nature and will realize that a dog is only what you make it; it mirrors you. Some people get dogs they don't deserve; hereditary faults play havoc with some dogs, and the poor owner can do nothing. I think if the faults are too great, it is kinder to put a bad dog to sleep after training and possibly veterinary advice have failed. There are so many wonderful dogs waiting for nice homes and understanding owners that, however difficult it may be to part with a dog, one that gives little pleasure and much trouble is not for the ordinary person to own.

Communication between the author and her dog, Millie.

It is useless expecting every dog of the same breed to turn out exactly the same. I don't expect the owner to remain the same throughout life, but of one thing I am absolutely certain—with sense, not psychiatry, the average owner can have a truly wonderful friend and companion in a dog. Remember, "dog" spelled backward is "god," and you should be "god" to your dog.

10·The Most Common Mistakes Made by Dog Owners

SOME OWNERS ARE OVERSENTIMENTAL. Love is one thing; sentimentality is another. Some dogs yelp when corrected when not in any way hurt. I proved this to one dog owner by kissing her dog, which yelped in exactly the same way as it did when corrected; I didn't think my kiss was that lethal! Dogs like firm commands and loving praise when they do right.

Owners use unkind thin-linked choke chains and jerk them upward instead of downward to correct a dog, and forget to take the left hand off the lead immediately after the jerk to allow the choke chain to release itself. They also jerk the lead with the palm of the hand facing upward instead of downward; this closes the choke chain on the dog's neck, and this may spoil the hair and is not kind. Choke chains of my pattern should never close on the neck. Owners forget to say, "What a good dog" when praising. The word "what" has a magical effect on the dog and usually produces an instant happy rapport and obedience.

"Sit, stay!" Signals should be given firmly from the shoulder.

Owners' signals are ineffective or muddling; they give them bending forward, so that the signal could be missed by the dog. Signals should be given firmly from the shoulder when standing upright. The hand giving the signal should be held away from the body so the dog can see the signal clearly.

Owners often "string up" show dogs on nylon leads; this must hurt the dog, because nylon leads have sharp edges. Dogs should be trained to stand and look alert on the command "Talk," which in my school means allowing a judge to handle a dog without its moving.

If a dog can't hold its head up naturally, in my opinion it is not worth an award.

Owners fail to realize that if they use firm, confident, kind jerks and a happy tone of voice, most dogs can be cured of nerves in a few hours. Never sympathize with a nervous dog; jerk it on gaily, speaking to it in a happy voice, using my thick-linked choke chain and, above all, have a four-foot lead held loosely over the two middle fingers of the right hand. Never close the right hand on the lead. A tight lead makes a dog nervous and dependent on its owner's support. When showing a dog, stand at least eighteen inches away from it to give it confidence on being handled by a judge. Owners should move fast when running a nervous dog; its tail then has to come up to balance it, and the habit grows and a natural tail carriage is established.

This is the correct position for jerking with the left hand when training the dog on the lead.

Owners fail when wishing a dog to be friendly or to be examined by a judge, to give the command "Go and talk," at the same time pointing at the person the dog has to acknowledge or be handled by. Without this training the nervous dog may be suspicious of anyone approaching and may back away. This especially applies to judges in the show ring who may be wary of approaching a dog who doesn't appear too friendly. The dog must be taught to stand still on the command "Stand" and look up wagging its tail, if possible, at whoever is pointed at by the handler when given this "talk" command. Owners have far too little range of voice tones. One needs low tones for commands given in a clear, firm voice. Higher, exuberant tones for praise when the dog has done well. A hard "no nonsense" tone for wrongdoing with deliberate disobedience.

Owners may still believe that a female's bad temperament is improved by her having puppies; this is not so—she just passes the bad temperament on to her puppies. They may also believe that to mate an oversexed dog makes it better; this is also a fallacy—it makes its behavior much worse, and it may even become bad-tempered with other dogs into the bargain.

Owners often don't realize that male and female human beings each have a different scent to a dog's nose so that one often hears that dogs won't let men handle them. This may easily be true, as dogs know men from women by this different scent. A normal dog either likes or dislikes both men and women, not one sex.

Individual men and women are attractive to dogs—why, we just don't know. I've often noticed that people who profess to be great dog lovers may not be liked by dogs, curious though it may be. I feel this is because they rush in too fast before the dog has time to sum them up. The holding out of one hand for the dog to smell in my opinion is the worst possible way to approach a dog: it shows the dog you do not feel confident that it will like you. I always approach a dog from the side if it is nervous and stand beside it, then take the lead and make it walk with me.

Dog owners often think that dog experts can solve their problems over the phone where temperament faults exist in the dog. This is rarely so; the owner has to be met and summed up. They also hope if they send their dog away to be trained it will return and obey them; in my opinion, this is utterly wrong, for it is the owner who needs the training much more than the dog. Many dogs sent away have returned dirty in the house, infected with a kennel cough and not obeying the owner. Some may have become nervous and may have lost faith in the owner.

11 · The Mind of the Dog

"PSYCHIATRY" IS DEFINED in the dictionary as "the study of mental disorders"; "psychoanalysis" as "the treatment of nervous ailments in which the causes are traced to forgotten concepts in the mind." This quickly damns psychoanalysis as being applicable to dogs, and the psychiatrist as assuming that all naughty or difficult dogs are so because of mental disorders. If this is the case I reckon that at least a million of our dogs alive today should be hastily destroyed, as psychoanalysis is impossible with dogs since they cannot answer questions and the concepts of their minds cannot be recalled and probed and changed, cast out or anything else.

This does not mean that anyone cannot understand the working of the dog's mind or thoughts, however you wish to put it, for telepathy on the part of dog and owner plays a vast part in the happy companionship between dog and mankind. Hundreds of times in my life I have shown in public that I know exactly what a dog is thinking at a certain moment, but I utterly refuse to believe that anyone knows what it was thinking in the past, and this is essential to the skill and work of a psychiatrist.

People are gullible. Invent a big word, charge high fees and, with the help of a working knowledge of dogs, one can get away with murder. A human personality can be so powerful that it can make a dog do and think things almost by hypnotism, just as a good actress can carry the audience to the height of happiness or despair with the part she is playing. But when the curtain drops, the atmosphere fades and the audience returns to its mundane affairs. That is why I have refused and shall continue to refuse to take dogs to train without their owners. I know I can make a dog do almost exactly as I wish when alone with it. Without the disturbing mental reactions of the owner, the dog is mine in will and thought.

But will a dog that carries out orders with armylike precision for me, with evident joy on its face, do the same for an owner who may be out of tune with the dog, either from lack of experience or sympathy, or from being just plain stupid, conceited or pigheaded? I know it won't. Then the partnership is doomed from the start. The dog becomes unsure of itself, the owner becomes unsure of the dog, and the trainer becomes unsure of both. He is sure only of the necessity for the owner to train himself or herself as much as the dog.

I have heard a thousand times a year the complaint "I have had dogs all my life, but this one is so different," often with the added remark, "You are my last hope. If you can't train him, I'll put him to sleep." That very remark appalls me when the poor dog is often only a puppy and his crime consists in tearing up furniture or biting the children or adults in the house or barking or whining incessantly. The owners have completely failed to find out what is the most likely cause of the trouble. They tear off to the veterinarian, who may have little experience in the training of dogs, for his job is their health. Often the advice given by the vet is not what a trainer would give. Tranquilizers, for instance, only mask the real fault, and, in the end, the owner realizes that the dog must either be trained or be put to sleep. Tranquilizers can only be a temporary measure to give the owner rest or confidence or both. For the dog they mean a dulling of its mind and body, but more about these later.

What governs the behavior of a dog? How far does its mind

think? What can be put down to instinct? I think that before a puppy is eight weeks old, instinct is nearly 99 percent of the dog's mind, and the control of its actions is almost entirely guided by the desire to eat, sleep, keep warm and play. After that the human contacts it makes, the discipline it receives, and the affection it develops for the person who nurtures it, begin to play an important part in the forming of the dog's mind and character.

No two people are alike; no two dogs are alike. We often see in the same litter an almost entirely different makeup in character and looks. Although it helps to study pedigrees and see the parents of the dog you are going to take into your home, there is no guarantee that a dog will be much like the last dog you had with similar breeding, or even like the rest of the litter he was born into. This is where owners trip up badly. They feel gypped if the breed that was previously a joy to them lets them down. They assume, for example, that all Border terriers are easily trained, affectionate and nice to own. They get extremely annoyed if their small puppy bites them, or won't come when called or maybe is dirty in the house, when their previous one made none of these mistakes. From the moment of his first blunder the dog hasn't quite the same loving owner as he had when he was purchased, and he subconsciously picks up the irritation of his owner by telepathy. He becomes aggressive because the owner is not feeling too well disposed toward him, and a vicious circle is started in more senses than one.

To train a dog with sympathy and understanding, one must try to understand a dog's mind. That mind has several big thoughts, its body a few major requirements. Firstly, the body governs the mind to a great extent when the puppy is young. The needs to eat, sleep, urinate and defecate are the main factors. It hasn't entered a dog's mind that it is wrong to puddle on the floor or soil its bed. Its reactions are entirely spontaneous. When scolded for these things it does not at first connect its action with the cross words and fear enters its mind. Nature's reactions to fear are many: some animals crouch and stay as still as if they were dead; others snarl and attack the thing or person that frightens them; others turn up their tummies believing this age-old action of a baby animal will help them; some urinate and move their bowels with seemingly no control whatsoever. Most young animals rush to drink from their mothers if frightened.

In training dogs, we must take all these things into consideration before we punish a dog and look upon him with disappointment or disgust. Only by repetition do dogs know what is right or wrong when very tiny. Their minds cannot reason what is right or wrong. They learn from experience of the tone of voice of the owner, or the jerk on a choke chain, or by being put into their kennels when naughty or any other punishment that the owner has thought to be suitable. But whatever the punishment, it is not always effective, for one has to gauge the natural reaction of the dog's mind to the treatment it is receiving or is about to receive. In many instances this reaction is to bite the person that is reproving it, or to lick and jump up on the person who is praising it. That is why, in my school, I am very loath to correct a keen and loving dog from jumping up in the early stage of training, for if you repress its natural exuberance and show of affection in the only way the dog knows, you may also be inhibiting the dog's natural love for you.

I think this love is of paramount importance, and I constantly hug, kiss and play joyfully with my pupils even if I have had to be extremely firm with them to achieve initial obedience. The result is that there enters the dog's mind a memory of affection and fun rather than fear of correction. For, make no mistake, dogs don't object to fair correction. In fact, if you face up to it, the most loving dogs often seem to belong to owners to whom I would hate to be related in any way. A dog longs for love and may think that by fawning on a horrid owner it may achieve its desire, and so he keeps on fawning *ad infinitum.* But woe betide the owner who refuses to face up to the fact that a dog's mind is not a human mind and firmly believes that any correction given to the dog will be remembered by that dog forever and held against the owner.

The dog has an enviable mind; it remembers the nice things in life and quickly blots out the nasty. That is why, when people tell me their small puppy was attacked by a big dog and that in later life made him into a fighter, I say, "Bunkum!" If your dog wasn't a fighter by nature, he wouldn't be one. Forget the past and deal with the present. Face up to the fact that his hormone balance or his hereditary characteristics are far more likely to make him into a fighter than having been attacked by another dog. After all, in the wild state, dogs were always attacking each other, and even play among dogs consists in biting and knocking each other over. Lack of firmness and leadership by the owner is far more likely to cause emotional upsets in a dog than a previous attack by another dog.

12 · Love, Honor and Obey

IN A DOG'S MIND, a master or a mistress to love, honor and obey is an absolute necessity. The love is dormant in the dog until brought into full bloom by an understanding owner. Thousands of dogs appear to love their owners, they welcome them home with enthusiastic wagging of the tail and jumping up, they follow them about their houses happily and, to the normal person seeing the dog, the affection is true and deep. But to the experienced dog trainer this outward show is not enough. The true test of real love takes place when the dog has got the opportunity to go out on its own as soon as a door is left open by mistake and it goes off and often doesn't return for hours. That dog loves only its home comforts and the attention it gets from its family; it doesn't truly love the master or mistress as they fondly think. True love in dogs is apparent when a door is left open and the dog still stays happily within earshot of its owner. For the owner must be the be-all and end-all of a dog's life.

To achieve this the owner has to master the dog at some time or other as the leader of the pack did in bygone days. There must be no question as to who is the boss of the house; it must be the owner. Dogs not only love owners who have had at one time a battle of wills for supremacy; they adore them, for a dog is really a subservient creature by nature, longing to trust his true love to someone's heart.

Now we come to the word "honor," or, as I prefer it, "respect." This respect in a dog's mind is paramount, and I can't repeat often enough that without respect, which includes a certain amount of "righteous fear," as the Bible would say, the dog lacks something in his essential makeup which sentimentality cannot replace.

When I use the term "righteous fear," women in particular shrink with horror; they wouldn't like their dogs to be afraid of them. When I explain that righteous fear is not being frightened, they don't understand. The reason humans don't all steal, lie or what have you, is simply that in most of us there is a righteous fear of the results. In dogs it should be the same. If they run off or fight another dog, their minds must be educated to know that there will be a reprisal, and without this righteous fear, the dog will never be completely happy, for dogs love looking up to their owners or, as the case may be, their trainers.

It is indeed very sad for me to see the number of dogs whose minds are forever tuned in to mine in a class when they should be tuned in to their owners' thoughts and wishes. The reason is, I make them immediately do as I wish and then give abundant praise. Many owners, in a distorted sense of kindness, let the dogs get away with disobedience, or make them obey so slowly that there is no respect for the owner from the dog. In fact many dogs show this in no mean way by biting their owners. When a dog bites its owner I feel sure it is mostly done as a last desperate resort to rouse the owner into being someone the dog can respect. Once the owner has got that respect, the dog can be taught everything with the least possible number of scoldings or corrections. A dog loves to learn things and adores to please. Once the hurdle of respect has been jumped, the continuation of training goes smoothly.

This sequence of events is very hard to teach dog owners, for a vast number of them have no idea what their dog prefers. They think dogs adore sentimentality. Dogs do up to a certain point, but even the tiniest of toy dogs wants a proper owner to love and

Dogs will do anything in the world for the owners they love.

respect; he may weigh only two pounds, but that does not mean he has no character or that he should not be obedient. People are now finding out that the tiniest Yorkshire terrier, for example, has a brain big enough to learn first-class obedience; its mind works the same as a Great Dane's mind, and it also wants to respect its owner. There is no difference between men owners and women owners regarding oversentimentality. In fact, I have found some men to be more stupidly sentimental than women, and when I have to be firm with their dogs they feel very bad about it. Yet the dogs show which they prefer, and every time it is the strong-minded but loving handler who gets real love and implicit obedience from the dog.

If a dog is cringing and frightened I always know that the owner has not been firm enough with it, for this type of dog needs someone to respect more than any other; it is weak-natured itself and likes to draw courage and strength from a firm owner.

What do I mean by the word "firm"? I use it so often that people may think I mean, "Get a stick and beat the dog." This is far from my mind. In fact, I think owners should practically never smack a dog, for it is a sign of defeat on the owner's part. It means that the dog's progressive training and the development of its mind and intelligence have not been accomplished. It means the owner has to resort to something that may be beyond his own strength. It is degrading for both dog and owner, for a dog that has been firmly but kindly trained never needs a beating. No, firmness in my estimation means a firmness of purpose, a strength of will that doesn't take defeat however long it takes to succeed. A firmness that is gentle as well as strong, for, make no mistake, a disobedient and willful dog needs prolonged patience and perseverance to win.

By being firm I mean giving the dog something to do and making him do it, knowing in your own mind that that which you wish him to do is fair and right and necessary for his and your happy coexistence. He may fight, scream as if being murdered, or just bite you in retaliation; or he may just seem mortally afraid—all these ruses can be tried by a dog when asked to obey. If you are not firm your inner heart revolts at making him obey and you are sorry for his whimperings or his apparent fear or defiance. You let up and let him get his own way. The seeds of disrespect are sown and will accordingly germinate, to the ultimate misery of both owner and dog.

Often in my class I meet these disrespectful dogs who don't truly love their owners. But the owners are mightily annoyed when I tell them their dogs don't really love them. They assure me the dog never leaves them in the house, etc., but that cuts no ice with me. I know that once I have shown the owners how much their dogs prefer me to them after I have made them carry out my wishes, they will be converted. I think the old adage "You have to be cruel to be kind" should be changed for dog owners to "You have to be firm to be kind." Firmness has to be continued only until the right kind of respect enters the dog's mind. And when the handler is being firm, unending praise and affection must be given to the dog.

Giving praise and affection is where a multitude of owners fail their dogs. A pat and a kind word are not enough in the initial training of dogs; the atmosphere must be charged with a certain excitement, for dogs are very sensitive to excitement; when they have done right, they love having the wildest show of affection and a good romp. Dull owners make dull dogs; stony-faced owners, zip-lipped owners and inhibited owners tend to have dull, disobedient dogs who take a long time to learn obedience.

As comedy makes up a big part of a child's life, it should do the same in a dog's life. Dogs love laughter, clapping and jokes. I had a little dog who laughed when we laughed although she hadn't the slightest idea what she was laughing about. It was the happiness that pervaded the room when we were laughing that entered her brain and made her feel happy so she laughed too. Try smiling at everyone you meet down the street; you will be amazed how many complete strangers smile back before they zip up again, realizing they don't know you. It is the same with dogs even if they don't know you; they respond to a smile and a clap if they have done well. They watch your eyes and face for the happy sign that you are pleased. I am intensely sorry for the dogs who see no smiles on their owners' faces. You can't train a dog well if you are unhappy; your tenseness communicates itself to the dog, and the dog becomes depressed.

What a wonderful indicator of happiness is the dog's tail; the half-mast wag with the very tip of the tail, showing nervous expectation; the half-mast slow wag of the interested dog who wants to know what master is saying but doesn't quite pick it up; the full-mast wag of excitement and happiness when he is really happy; and last but not least, the tail between the legs of the nervous, shy or unhappy dog who trusts no one and to whom life is a burden.

When a dog is happily learning, or happily obeying, I like to see its tail at the medium sensible height; when having a game after

"What I like most is to change in a matter of minutes the tail between the legs to the half-mast. . . ."

lessons or when free I like the full mast. But what I like most is to change in a matter of minutes the tail between the legs to the half-mast by firm and sensible handling, for this can be done if you get through to the dog's mind and give strength to it by your own forceful happiness and strength of purpose. A dog that loves, honors and consequently obeys is a joy to himself and his owner.

13 · Sex

Everyone who has a lot to do with the training of dogs can't help noticing that females are far easier to train than males. The reason is that, except when she is "in heat" or in the throes of a pseudopregnancy, a female's attention is not disturbed by matters of sex—although greyhounds are not raced within three months after being in heat, because they are supposed not to be at their best at those times. A bitch is better-tempered than a male dog on the whole, for the fighting instinct for supremacy over other dogs is not so prevalent, although females do become extremely jealous, especially of their own offspring. I have known mother and daughter to fight incessantly, so that one had to be parted with. This often happens in the human race—with mother and daughter not getting along—so it is not surprising to us to find it in the animal kingdom as well. Sex is a thing no so-called psychiatrist can fathom, for the dog again cannot answer questions as to whether his sex life is normal or whether he had unpleasant sexual adventures when young. Therefore the dog owner must rely on experience of sexual behavior in dogs and use that knowledge to make the dog's existence healthy and happy.

Many dogs literally seem to have minds preoccupied almost entirely with sex for most of their lives. These oversexed dogs are a curse to themselves and their owners; they are abnormal and should not, in my opinion, perpetuate the race, for in these days of crowded urban and suburban areas and lack of a free run for dogs, an oversexed dog is a curse. You can't get through to their minds at all without intensive training for long periods and with a greater degree of firmness than, in my opinion, is kind. I say with all my heart that unless the owner of this dog particularly requires it for show purposes, it should be neutered to make its life happy and that of its owners equally trouble-free. Wild cries of "I wouldn't like to do that to my dog," or "I would hate to take its nature away" are bound to be heard from ignorant people who know little about altering animals, whose vets have meager or no personal experience of it, or from people who know someone who knows someone who had his dog done and it got fat and dull. What they didn't bother to find out was what the owner of the altered dog was like. Did that owner feed the dog every time it asked for food? Did that owner reduce the food he had been giving it, as it was no longer using up energy fussing over sex matters? Did that owner give it reasonable exercise and sufficient training to make its life interesting? These are the factors that make an altered dog no different from any other dog except that it is happier in every way and a joy to own in town or country, with or without other dogs. Only when sex is a nuisance need this be done, and I heartily recommend it to everyone whatever the age of the oversexed dog.

What goes on in the mind of the oversexed male dog? The answer is, Nothing but the desire to copulate. It doesn't really matter whether the bitch it meets is in heat; it often doesn't matter whether the dog it meets is male or female; it is quite happy to carry out its sexual exercises on the leg of a child or even the furniture. It growls ferociously at other dogs, willing to fight any of them because of nervous sexual excitement; it often bites its owner in a fit of frustration. It barks or whines most of the day and cannot at any time be made to attend with proper concentration when there are other dogs about, whatever their sex. Many people think they will cure this oversexed menace by letting him "have a bitch." How sorry they will be if they do this! All the full flood of sexual fulfillment makes the dog a maniac after such an encounter, for now his instincts are more fully aroused than ever and discipline may become almost impossible. Yet get this dog alone in some place where no dog has been, and no smells or dogs are about, and he will often be the nicest possible dog, happy, loving and obedient.

Why then are owners so hesitant about altering dogs? Over four hundred dogs have been altered on my advice, and in every case the owner and dog are happy, where formerly the dog was impossible, the owner fed up and the partnership in grave danger of being ended. My owners take my advice as to a strict diet and continue the training of their dog, for neutering takes time to work until all the hormones already manufactured in the dog's body are exhausted; but even after three weeks most owners note a difference. The normal male dog shows no interest in a female not in heat and only cursory interest in a female in heat for her first week; he shows no interest in mounting other male dogs, furniture or people's legs and will leave smells and lamp posts alone when trained in obedience. He is seldom a fighter.

There have been dogs that are unstable because they are hermaphrodite; that is, they have two sexes in one body. This causes dogs to be bad-tempered and unreliable, as are the male dogs known as "monorchids" or "cryptorchids," meaning that only one or neither of their testicles have descended into the scrotum. Neutering in these cases is difficult and a major operation. In normal cases it is a simple and uneventful operation done by an experienced vet; no stitches need be used, and the dog can return home in less than twenty-four hours.

A neutering operation does not adversely affect a dog's mind. There must be no ideas in the owner's head about denying the dog its natural pleasures; an ordinary dog doesn't get those "natural pleasures" unless it is a stud dog or belongs to a bad owner who allows it to wander and have promiscuous relations with any bitch it meets. Dogs who have no desires don't fret because they have lost those desires; they love their owners more dearly; they are spirited, happy dogs, not deluded miseries cursed by too great an abundance of hormones.

After all, sex in a dog cannot be looked upon in the same way as sex in humans. Dogs don't have sex hormones for any other reason than to perpetuate the race and, with this object in mind, males will get thin and miserable when a bitch is in heat in the neighborhood; will travel miles, making their feet sore, in spite of hunger and thirst, to wait hopelessly outside a bitch's home; will take even a beating without noticing it in the attempt to attack or carry out sex impulses with other male dogs; and will destroy floors or furniture or other appointments in sexual frustration. The mind of a dog doesn't look into the future if its sex organs are to be removed; it doesn't anticipate a loss of pleasure; it has a general anesthetic so knows nothing about the operation. Three or four days later nobody would know the dog had had anything done to it except that it remains the same happy dog it always was and becomes more interested in the odd snack between meals!

With female dogs this characteristic of being oversexed doesn't exist; the spaying of bitches, except in case of disease, is not to be lightly recommended from my experience. It is a more serious operation than alteration for a male dog; the bitch does become less lively, and there is a tendency to get fat. This does not mean that I think every bitch should breed a litter for her health. I think that utterly wrong. It has been proved in veterinary circles that female dogs bred are more susceptible to uterine disease than those not bred. Many oversentimental people worry when their pets, obviously keen to mate, fret a bit and, although puppies are not wanted, they mate her "for her own sake, bless her." I think they are wrong. There are too many unwanted dogs today to warrant breeding for this reason.

Only females and males with some special points should be bred and never if the animal's temperament is bad. Breeding will not make a bad-tempered or shy female or male dog better-tempered or social; all that is being done is passing on to unfortunate dog owners a bad-tempered animal. This particularly applies to owners of breeds whose temperament has been deteriorating in so many cases.

If a dog is mentally unhappy with its sex and shows it by fussing at all times about other dogs, neuter it. You are being kind, not cruel, to the dog and all who meet it.

No psychiatrist can help the dog by mind reading. Sex is above all that nonsense. Firm training can do a lot, but take an experienced trainer's advice. No dog-loving trainer will tell you your dog is oversexed if it only lacks training.

14 • Praise

THE MIND OF A DOG IS forever open to taking in, by touch, by telepathy, and by talking, the feelings, ideas, emotions and wishes of its owner. That is, if the dog loves its owner. To get through to a dog's mind you don't need a couch and sweet music or probing questions from a psychiatrist. You need hands that on touching the dog send messages of love and sympathy to its brain. You need a voice with a wide range of tones to convey aurally your wishes and feelings toward the dog. You need eyes that tell the dog who watches them what you are feeling toward it, even though the message may be hidden from the outside world. Above all, you need telepathy so that the dog thinks with you.

These things are not always born in people. They can be developed as any sense or gift can be developed. That is, providing the person who wishes to develop them is honest in mind, because with animals you cannot cheat; it is useless watching a trainer handling your dog with hatred of her in your heart, or dislike of all the things she is doing which you think unnecessary or harsh or both. If you give an order to your dog by word of mouth and are feeling sorry for it inside you are doomed to failure. Dogs above all creatures love honesty of purpose. If you pat a dog and your fingers are not carrying that loving message you don't deceive the dog.

No one knows why touch is so important. I think probably blind people know more than any of us about the sensitivity of touch;

The author with future guide dogs.

that is why guide dogs are usually so faithful. But the ordinary handler can develop this touch which calms the wild dog, which produces ecstasy in dogs when you caress them, but it has to come through the fingers or face direct from your heart. In every training school the words "Praise your dog" are heard constantly; by those words in my school I don't necessarily mean a big, hearty pat. I mean a communion of brain and touch. I lay my face alongside that of the dog with its face cupped in my hands, and I sense that my deep love and admiration for it passes right through to its mind, often in silent communion, for I have already said, "What a good dog" and clapped my hands to show approval at the end of the exercise. But a dog needs more than that if you are to get its complete mind in tune with yours. Unhappy are the handlers who think this all stuff and nonsense. For it makes dogs truly happy.

Lots of dogs have to put up with second-best praise, but if you can't let yourself go, you must at least mean what you say when praising. The tone of voice must convey great joy to the dog. It must convey to him that you think him the most wonderful dog on earth, and you must never mind what other people in the school are thinking. Half the trouble in training schools is the natural restraint and reserve that stifles people in public. They cannot forget themselves; they cannot abandon themselves to working and praising or correcting the dog.

In the same way, it is difficult for most of us to correct our dog in the street for fear of what people will do or say or think. If we truly love our dog, other people and their thoughts won't matter, but it is easier to write this than to carry it out. The general public is so ill informed on the training of dogs that I am certain the A.S.P.C.A. gets a multitude of phone calls from oversentimental ignoramuses who haven't the foggiest idea what goes on in a dog's mind and think it cruel to correct a dog firmly. They confuse discipline with cruelty and apparently would rather see a dog run over or put to sleep than have it corrected in the street when it has done wrong. But the handler's life is almost in danger if he corrects a dog in public in the effort to make it eligible for praise.

It is extraordinary how dogs pick up praise straight from your brain almost before you have had time to put it into words. A dog's mind is so quick in picking up your thoughts that, as you think them, they enter the dog's mind simultaneously. I have great difficulty in this matter in giving the owners commands in class, for the dog obeys my thoughts before my mouth has had time to give the owner the command. I find it extremely difficult to correct a dog for this, although it shouldn't really be obeying me; it should be tuned in to the owner, who of course doesn't know what I am going to say until I have said it—that is, unless the owner is also telepathic.

In the same way, I know what the dog is thinking as it thinks and can often therefore stop it from being naughty or disobedient before it has erred. This spares the necessity of correcting it and helps speed up the training. But I find the chattering that goes on in class by those people who don't truly concentrate very hampering to this mind communication. It is like constant interference on a radio. But then I don't suppose many people know what a thrill it is to be on the same wavelength as a dog.

Praise can be given in so many ways—by tidbits for a puppy, by tone of voice, by scratching a dog's chest, by firm, warm pats on the back, by kissing, which all dogs love, or by just looking straight into their eyes and smiling. You can't deceive dogs. It doesn't matter whether you say "Good dog" or "Gadzooks." The dog knows what you mean.

15 · Correction

THE CORRECTING OF A DOG inevitably gives more pain to the owner than it does to the animal; the resulting effect on the mind is far worse for the owner than for his pet. Dogs are the most wonderful creatures to own because they don't brood about the past, they don't hold a grudge against their owners, they seem to know when correction is fair and just, and they definitely have consciences, which to me proves they also have souls, although I am told this is not possible and in the next world we shall not see our dogs again!

This book is not to help those dogs for whom a pained look is enough to make them crawl in shame, nor those who listen for the sad tone of voice which denotes the owner's displeasure. Rather it is for those dogs whom the owners erroneously thought psychiatry could help. The dogs we are dealing with are problems in some way, and the more gentle and persuasive treatment is unlikely to work on them.

What can a handler do and what is the effect on a dog's mind? First of all, I believe most correction can be accomplished with a sharp jerk on the choke chain providing the choke chain is the thick-linked variety, not the watch-chain type, which is cruel. This jerk has a wonderful effect on a dog; it does not pain him, but it shocks his mind into thinking, and a shock, however caused, is much more likely to be remembered than a scolding. Everyone knows in medical practice these days shock treatment by electric impulses is given to nervously unstable patients. I believe that the same sort of thing happens to nervously unstable dogs when jerked hard on a choke chain. I have cured the most cringing, terrified dogs in a matter of minutes, not days, with a few sharp jerks, the cupping of my hands around their faces and a lot of cheerful encouragement.

One boxer got a first prize with the report "What a wonderful temperament." Had the judge seen this dog three days previously she would have had to lie on the floor to inspect it. The owner was horrified when she saw me jerk her kennel star but was soon won over when she saw the almost instantaneous response. I have seen nervous Alsatians, terrified of everyone and dirty in the house because they were too nervous outside to perform their duties, become sound in mind and consequently immediately clean in the house when cured of nerves by this method.

After much thought I have decided that the effect of correction on a dog's mind is to give it confidence, a happy respect for its handler and a longing to be with the person who carries out the correction. No one quite knows why some dogs are excessively nervous. Even when there are faultless pedigrees showing no hereditary nerves or viciousness, these pathetic creatures are born. People despair and put them to sleep, when really there is absolutely no need for this if they can be cured in hours. They obviously have inner horrors such as fearing to jump into a car; being terrified of going upstairs, horrified at the sight of a man or a woman or a child, none of whom has ever done the dog harm. I get hundreds of letters from people who assume that this fear is due to possible ill treatment in the past, but this is most unlikely; few people really ill-treat a puppy. I know it to be mostly nervous instability, cause unknown.

Most people who have these nervous dogs coax them, sympathize with them, don't go in cars if the dog doesn't wish to accompany them, don't make the dog go upstairs if it is frightened, don't make it talk to men or children if frightened, and generally put up with a lot of unhappy inconvenience to, as they think, help the dog. This has a disastrous effect on the dog's mind, for he picks up the sad sympathy of the owner's mind, feels the gentle pull on the lead when he won't walk on it, and senses the nervous tension of the owner struggling to help him. The terror gets worse and worse, and the owner usually, on a vet's or an incompetent trainer's advice, puts the unhappy dog to sleep when, in many cases, it has had less than twelve months of life.

My heart bleeds for these misguided owners and their dogs. If only they knew how easy it is to change these nervous dogs, they would be happier. But first they must understand a dog's mind. They must harden their hearts and realize that what they are going to do to the dog is for its good, in the same way as a surgeon cuts off a limb to save a life; he doesn't squirm at the ghastly business of chopping off the limb, he looks forward to the regaining of health and life in the patient. I treat dogs in the same way. I know if I can shut my ears to the occasional terrified squeaks of the terrified dog and continue without emotion to jerk it on, that in about ten to fifteen minutes, I shall have won. The dog will stop being frightened; the cure will have begun. It is then only a matter of teaching a dog routine exercises to strengthen its sense of security.

But my greatest problem is to get the owners in the right frame of mind. Some of them need shutting in somewhere away from the dog while the cure is going on; they should be released only when the dog is cured. But if you did this they would not see for themselves how the cure was carried out; they would not pick up the confident way the dog progressed, and, above all, they would not see the loving way the dog responds to the correct handling. Definitely this cure must be with the cooperation of owner and absolute trust in the trainer. Sometimes it is necessary to muzzle a very nervous dog since otherwise, in their initial fear, they may attempt to bite. This must never be allowed. The handler must be completely safe in carrying out his corrections, for the slightest fear on the part of the handler will undo all the good the jerking has done.

Many dogs object at first to a muzzle, and they struggle to get it off. The sentimental owner wrings her hands in suppressed sympathy. The atmosphere is charged with emotion, although really there is nothing cruel about a muzzle. Greyhounds wear them all the time when out. Dogs in Italy and other foreign countries wear them for protection against rabies. Many dogs with bad temperaments in this country would be far happier free with muzzles than kept snarling on a short lead. For while the dog is muzzled, the owner need not fear a fight, for a dog can do no harm in a well-fitting muzzle. I have muzzles that fit so that drinking and panting are in no way impeded. After a few minutes the dog doesn't worry about a muzzle, and usually under an hour later it can be discarded. Only for the initial safety of the handler and the dog is it occasionally necessary to use one.

The next type of correction is a good shake. The dog needs grasping by his choke chain and scruff on both sides of his neck under his ears, and while looking the dog straight in the eyes scold in a thunderous tone and give three or four hard shakes. This will calm a hysterical dog and will make a "don't care" one listen to you. It is a correction that makes the dog feel slightly silly, and he doesn't want it repeated. I have seldom had to shake a dog more than twice. This correction needs strength with a big dog, but it is of course a dog's own answer to unruliness in a dog pack. Dogs shake each other in play or fight, and when the handler does it, he is only being a better dog than the dog itself, which is an attitude all dogs respect.

Shutting a dog up and not speaking to it as a correction is quite stupid. The dog's mind doesn't understand this sort of correction at all. You can punish humans by sending them to solitary confinement; you can only lose a dog's deep affection by the same treatment. A dog's mind can't reason that because he ate the Sunday roast he is being shut up in the cellar or bathroom or not being spoken to. His simple mind will either fret for your companionship or he will go off to find something interesting to amuse him and end up by tearing up the floor or committing some other mischief.

The dog's mind is not to be compared with even a child's mind. His conscience acts only when he knows from long contact with his owner that he has done wrong. By the owner's attitude of mind he senses that he has done wrong, but correction must be given at the moment of the wrong action, because he won't remember later what he has done. That is why smacking a dog when he comes back to you after having run off for hours is useless. To him you are smacking him for coming to you—he doesn't remember that he ran off hours ago. That is why in my school I personally try to catch dogs running away from their owners and give them a whack with the end of a soft leather lead on their backsides. It is being caught in the action that teaches a dog. I hate any owner to smack a dog. Let me be the horrid person that has to do it if all calling fails.

What a dog's mind can interpret as a punishment is being put into the "down" position and being made to stay there until he feels more disposed to cooperate with his handler. This has a wonderful effect on hysterical dogs, barking dogs, fighting dogs and obstreperous dogs, and I strongly recommend that anyone with a naughty dog master the act of putting the dog into the down for short spells at a time. The dog is under control in the down, and his mind recognizes your mastery over him. Dogs like being mastered—it gives them a nice, safe feeling and of course makes them respect the handler.

Lastly, smacking a dog as a punishment is only to be used as a last resort and should be used if a dog, without rhyme or reason, attacks another dog or a person. The inflicting of pain on him at these attacks is an "eye for an eye" and is a quick and effective deterrent for a very serious crime. But the smacking should if possible be done with a leather lead over the dog's rump. Never hit a dog with a newspaper or on its face. No crime should ever involve a newspaper; it is ineffective and really annoys and hurts the dog's mind.

No dogs are permanently hurt in mind or body after three or four whacks with a leather lead, and I have known it to cure a fighter caught in the act of aggression. The whacking of a dog inevitably hurts the handler more than the dog, and those in poor health cannot do it. In my school no pupil is ever allowed to smack a dog. If it has to be done I do it myself—without temper and sufficiently hard to make the dog feel it without harming it at all. All dog lovers hate doing it or watching it being done, but in some

An effective correction: making the dog stay in the down position for short spells at a time.

cases dogs are so stubborn as to exhibit no finer feelings, and this is the only effective treatment. It may save them from being put to sleep.

In all cases of correcting a dog the handler's character has to be taken into consideration, for most dogs' faults are really handlers' faults, and the faults in handlers' temperaments are multitudinous. I think hundreds of them should never own a dog, but as there is no law that permits dogs to be taken away from stupid owners, the poor dog has to be made to conform to the owner whatever the owner's state of mind or condition, or his home surroundings. I am often terribly, terribly sorry for dogs that come to me. I long to keep them and give them a sensible existence, but all I can do is to make misfits fit as far as is within my power. At the end of many of my training sessions I almost need a psychiatrist myself!

16 • *Jealousy*

IN THE CASE OF JEALOUSY the mind of a dog works in almost an identical way to that of a human being. It wants the full attention and love of its owner whether the jealousy occurs only when another dog enters the home or when the beloved owner talks to another dog outside, or whether the jealousy is aimed at another person in the home. The same driving force is at the root of the evil in all of these cases—the intention of the dog to reign alone and supreme in his household.

The guarding instinct so prevalent in some breeds has its roots in the same sort of thing—a desire to let no one enter the precincts of his master or mistress. Jealousy nearly always takes the form of a show of viciousness toward the dog or person the animal is jealous of. Quite often it is a mild form of jealousy and only involves its bone, toy or the piece of rug that it is fond of. It jealously guards them and woe betide anyone trying to take that object away.

This jealousy is particularly pronounced when puppies are reared and kept in the household. As the puppy reaches the age of about three months the mother will begin to feel jealous as her maternal instinct fades and the time draws near for another heat. In spite of the attempt to treat both dogs equally and always to talk to both at the same time, feeding both at the same time and exercising both together, the jealousy continues to grow.

Correction works at first and then bit by bit grows less effective. In the dog's mind a usurper has entered the scene, and, as in the wild state, the dam is trying to turn the young out of the nest. As she fails to get rid of the now grown-up pup, her temper gets worse and worse in the effort to dislodge the now adult and unwanted member of the household. She becomes more and more thwarted as her owner attempts to make the newcomer as welcome as the old-established member. Often she will turn on her owner when he is trying to make peace, as if she were trying to impress an ignorant person that it was time the youngster went out into the world to fend for itself.

If you are a really good handler your training methods will be good enough to make both dogs obey the command "Leave" when they are in your presence. The danger lies in the times you leave the dogs together on their own, for the slightest boldness on the part of the youngster in approaching the older one's basket or toy, etc., will infuriate the older dog, and she will set on the youngster tooth and nail. Sometimes, unless kept apart from her offspring, the mother will try to kill it. Such is the age-old instinct to get rid of the young before it is time to breed again. Luckily this instinct is not very common. Generations of domesticity have dimmed it considerably, but I have met it, mostly in smaller dogs, and I am sorry to say that I have not been able to give the owners much hope of curing it.

Most dogs show a streak of jealousy at some time or other. When my own two dogs used to come to my bedroom, if I talked to the Dane the little English toy terrier would jump on the bed and nip at the Dane's nose even though she was smiling all the time so that her own face would receive the pats and kisses the big one was getting—and which she would also have got—but there was a streak of jealousy in her nature which did not appear in the Dane's. But then I think little dogs possess this factor in a more marked degree than big dogs, who are more placid.

Jealousy occurs when two terriers are hunting. If one catches a rat the other will often try to take it away, not because it wants it—most good ratters instantly leave their dead quarry to find other live ones—but simply because the dog is jealous and wants to be equal with the killer.

Biting of husbands or wives is a very common form of jealousy. The dog senses that he is not the be-all and end-all of a beloved mistress when the master of the house comes home, and therefore, if the husband goes near his wife, he may be bitten. The answer to this one is for the husband to master the dog in no mean way by leaving a string on its choke chain and, when it attempts to be nasty, giving it an almighty jerk and a scolding, then petting and loving it. Then the dog will recognize the man is the boss, and all dogs are happy to submit to a real master.

Few men dare do this with their wives' dogs for fear of upsetting their wives or, in some cases, of literally being attacked by their wives in defense of the dogs, for some wives would rather have their husbands bitten than allow the husbands to correct the dogs. How silly can some women be, for surely the life of the family depends on the happiness of all concerned and the dog is as much part of the family as a child. I encourage husbands to watch their wives training their dogs and sometimes to take over the training. It forms a happy camaraderie in the attempt to make the dog a "joy to all and a nuisance to no one."

In the curing of this husband-biting complex the wife must try to feel really annoyed if the dog attacks, for—make no mistake—a dog picks up the thoughts of the wife without a word being spoken, and if it thinks the wife doesn't really disapprove, the dog will continue to bite. But if she feels really angry about it and so does the husband, the combined waves of disapproval floating about for the dog's mind to pick up will be strong enough for even the most insensitive dog.

Correction by the mistress of the dog in these cases seems to fail, the reason being that the dog doesn't respect the person it is jealous of. Otherwise it would live in a peaceful coexistence. The person of whom the dog is jealous must do the correcting, and often this is an aged grandmother or grandfather who lacks the physical strength to handle the dog in the right way. Then there is little hope of a cure, and the dog must simply be kept out of the way of the person it is jealous of. It must not be the other way around, asking the person to keep out of the way. A human being must always come first in these matters, or the dog will realize it is supreme and become worse and worse as its ego gets stronger support.

Dogs are seldom jealous of small children. The mind of a dog looks upon small children as it would look upon its own whelps. That is why even fierce dogs are seldom known to hurt children.

A nervous dog is always a potentially dangerous dog. That is why I always curse the breeders who sell these creatures and who breed litters from problem dogs, hoping their traits won't come out in their offspring. This hope is not often fulfilled. Nervous parents teach their puppies fear by telepathy from an early age, and if the bitch feels fear, the puppies automatically follow suit. Only with training, from an early age if possible, will the fear be eradicated.

Jealousy in kenneled dogs is particularly rife in stud dogs. Each stud dog wants to reign supreme over the kennel wives, and when there are a number of stud dogs present, it is wise to keep them apart. Although dogs are polygamous by nature, they often choose a favorite wife. I clearly remember my Alsatian, Argus, choosing a wife and going off with her to our orchard and digging a fifteen-foot underground passage and bedroom at the end for her to have her litter in; his other wives were just for business purposes only, this one was the true mate. We allowed her to have her nine puppies down there, and seeing Argus standing erect on top of the entrance the day the mother whelped was a thrilling sight, for we felt the true nature of the dogs had been allowed to develop by choosing their own home and bringing up the babies in a homely atmosphere.

Only when the babies were fourteen days old and near to weaning time did we interfere. They were the most wonderful litter we had ever bred. I had never before met with instinct like that and I have never since. When we opened up the nest we saw that it was beautifully made around a corner of the passage, with straw and hay the bitch had picked up in her mouth, plus masses of her own hair she had plucked from her chest. The nest was scrupulously

A class of dogs—and their owners—trained by the author in only six and a half hours.

clean and dry; in fact, she was a model housekeeper, one that many human mothers could well emulate.

I don't believe there is any cure for jealousy in stud dogs. I think that if some of them had the chance, they would fight to the finish; and that is too near nature to enable the dog trainer to do an efficient job, although I do recommend muzzling and exercising them together if the breed is not too big. Naturally if dogs are properly obedience-trained from the start, problems like jealousy seldom occur, but the average breeder has no time or wish to carry out obedience training for fear it may spoil the character of the show dogs. Most trainers know that, far from spoiling the dog's character, obedience training enhances a dog's chance of achieving through perfect ring manners. I still hope the day will come when no working breed wins a championship title without also having obtained some simple obedience credentials.

A trained dog's mind is educated; the look on its face is quite different from that of the scatty brutes one often sees in the ring. It has an aura of warm, friendly confidence sadly lacking in many show dogs. Because it has supreme confidence in its handler it can rest quietly at a show if they have to be parted, and that counts for a lot when you need a dog at the peak of its form even after a tiring day. The mind of a dog can absorb so much that it is child's play for him to carry out obedience exercises on command and yet still remember to stand and be examined and to walk and run as required for the beauty ring. It only means that a few different commands are learned, and that is no difficulty for an intelligent dog. If it is not intelligent it shouldn't win prizes, for who wants a stupid dog with no mind of its own?

On the subject of jealousy, I think some of my pupils are a bit jealous themselves when I work their dogs and should realize that only by years of experience have I learned anything about the training of dogs; they cannot expect to work a dog without learning the art the hard way—that is, hard work, patience and the willingness to learn something new every day from someone. None of us knows it all, and the pupil who rushes in with a know-it-all attitude will not learn as quickly as those who watch and listen, eager to assimilate knowledge.

Every dog is different, and although they all may undergo identical training, it is only by reading their minds and watching their reactions that a handler may make progress. Most human pupils are wonderful the way they patiently try to follow suit in the training methods, and I think some of their dogs are absolutely beastly to be uncooperative to such loving owners, but a dog's nature is governed by a multitude of instinctual reactions and none of us really knows it all.

I have tried neutering for jealousy among male dogs not wanted for show or stud, and it doesn't work. This is the one vice it doesn't touch, which proves that jealousy is a mental thing, not a sexual one. If the dogs are both sent to boarding kennels or a trainer they will show no signs of jealousy and will live peacefully together again until such time as they adopt that place as home; then the trouble starts all over again. All of which goes to prove it is true jealousy as suffered by the human race, not lack of training or an hereditary fault.

17 • Fighting

FIGHTING DOGS ARE THE ONES that cause their owners the most worry. It is this vice that many owners hope a psychiatrist will be able to probe and cure, but once again I insist that since this is the process of investigating into the past of a dog's mind, which cannot be probed because the dog cannot answer questions, no progress can be made with psychiatry. That does not mean we cannot understand a dog's present state of mind. Although past events might have had disastrous effects on the dog and might have affected his mind and emotional makeup, it would have to be the owner who is psychoanalyzed to find the answer to the dog's problems. But because few owners would have the nerve or sense to go to a human doctor to find out why their dogs fight, I think we can leave out this subject too.

A dog fights for several reasons, usually the right to survive, whether this be taken as the right to eat and live peaceably or simply that the dog wants to live up to a certain standard whereby he has no enemies or neighbors that irritate him. We do not know which motive fits each individual case. What we do know is that dogs pretend to fight in play, mauling each other in a rough and tumble which nobody minds. Puppies have mock fights all the time to strengthen their limbs and develop their jaws and to wear off their superabundance of energy, but the subject we are looking at here is serious dog fighting, which is dangerous for dogs and humans and has been known to end in death for the smaller and weaker dog. Even if the fight is not so bad as to end in death it can cause the owner of a dog to have a heart attack from fear or people can be bitten. It is most unpleasant and terrifying, to say the least.

Most people don't realize it takes quite a minute for two dogs to get really to grips—before that they are playing for a hold. Therefore, when you go to separate a dogfight, there is no need to rush in and be bitten. It is far safer to watch at close range until you can safely get a hold of a collar or of the loose skin between the eyes of the dog. Once a dog has got a hold on another dog, it is unlikely that he will turn around and bite you for to do so he would have to release the other dog. You are reasonably safe when it has got a hold in slipping a lead on or grabbing the choke chain or scruff.

It is generally useless beating the dogs in a dogfight; they would be mentally unaware of pain at that moment, and unless you knocked either dog out you would not separate them once either had a real hold. A mild dogfight, where death is not the object of the aggressor, can sometimes be stopped by beating when a dog has no collar, but the best method if two people are around is for each on the word "now" to grab their collars and hold them off their front legs so they begin to choke. It takes terrific strength to do this with big dogs, so I grab the flesh on the forehead between the eyes and he will let go at once with this. Moreover, they cannot bite you.

What is in the dog's mind when it attacks every dog it meets or just has one enemy around the corner? Most of it is show of strength, very often a cowardly show of strength aimed at other people's toy dogs who can't answer a bully back. Face that same bully with a big dog likely to answer back and it will disappear into the distance, for the dog knows who will be boss even in its own race, and if it senses superiority of physique or brain, it will automatically be subservient. That is why young dogs lie on their backs, all four feet in the air, when they meet an older or stronger dog; they know who is boss and are showing the other dog so by giving the "pax" sign, which is exposing the tummy to an enemy. That is why I tell pupils that this trick is not a nice one really and should be checked at an early age, for it is purely one of a weak animal giving in to one stronger in mind and usually an enemy at that. Few owners would like to think their dogs look upon them as enemies, but that is the case. When a dog no longer looks upon you as a potential enemy it stops this lying on its back as protection, although many dogs in later life do it because their owners have scratched their chests, which they like, and they hope for it again. But primarily it belongs to the defense mechanism of the dog tribe.

The mind of a dog that fights always has at the back of it the wish to be the boss of the tribe, and he fights other male dogs who are sexually mature to make sure there is no risk of his being questioned as "lord of all he surveys." Muzzle that dog and let him loose with the dog he has previously fought and nine times out of ten he will realize he is at a disadvantage and show no signs of aggression. That is why I muzzle fighters and free them with trained dogs or nonfighters. They then learn to enjoy themselves in a community and the wish to fight goes. Often, having muzzled, introduced and trained them for a short time together, I have formerly bad fighters lying side by side without muzzles after a few minutes.

Your own personality needs to be strong to deal with fighters, because fighters are usually adult dogs. Few puppies fight, few bitches fight; therefore your mind must be stronger than that of the potential fighter so that you are the boss, not either of the dogs. If the dog is sex-mad you can do nothing but neuter it. Muzzling is only a stopgap, not a cure. Owners who won't have their fighting dogs neutered should always have them muzzled in public places. There is nothing so terrifying as having one's well-trained dog attacked. My dog was attacked in the post office when put to the sit, and she did not answer the boxer who had attacked her. I really suffered from shock after it, as I think anyone would seeing his or her own much beloved pet victimized by an untrained bully, coupled with the physical effort needed to drag a fully adult male boxer off one's dog. Had my dog been a fighter I do not believe I would have had the strength to keep them apart when separated, and few people will help you in such emergencies.

I think owners of fighting dogs should be prosecuted if their dogs are ever allowed free unmuzzled in public places. I know of several cases where innocent poodles have had severe injuries and one of a dear little female fox terrier whose leg was broken by boxers in a London park. That little dog will never be well. The boxers live to do it again; their owners are quite irresponsible.

Many dogs that fight are undoubtedly mentally unsound, just as mad as human beings in lunatic asylums. But there are no lunatic asylums for dogs, only trainers who must know, if they are honest, that many of these dogs are incurable and that all the training or sentiment in the world won't help them. If firm training and/or neutering doesn't stop them, I think they should be put to sleep, muzzled when out or never brought into contact with other people's dogs. I have met few really mad dogs; with the right instruction and veterinary treatment, I have advised only about twenty of my dog pupils be put to sleep out of seventeen thousand.

Jealousy, sex and the guarding instinct are the three things that cause most fights; the dog's mind runs only on those lines unless he is starving and fighting for food, unlikely in this year of grace for dogs belonging to readers of this book. The cure is firm handling and training, neutering in really bad cases, and the treatment of the dog by freeing it with other nonfighting dogs under supervision.

The breeders of fighting dogs should be heavily punished because quite a bit of the problem is hereditary. No fighter should win a prize in any show.

One can usually read the signs that a dog is about to fight seconds before it attacks—the stiffening of the legs, the raising of the hair along the back, the springy gait as if the dog were on hot bricks, and the slightly curved walk forward which means the dog is ready to turn instantly should his foe attack his hindquarters. If you are tuned in to your dog's mind you will pick up by telepathy the tenseness before any of the visible signs appear. If you are exercising a fighter you should always be on the *qui vive.* A thunderous command "Leave" often brings a dog to its senses and no fight occurs.

18 · Food

TO WHAT EXTENT DOES food govern a dog's mind? This is a question that most owners have had to face at one time or another, and many of them have told me they think food occupies most of the waking and thinking hours of their dogs. But I am quite sure that the people who own such dogs are very unlucky.

The hunting instinct is extremely strong in most dogs; therefore, with problem dogs that chase and kill chickens or other livestock, the act is only what nature taught them to do many thousands of years ago. Their noses were designed for tracking down and killing, and although domesticity has vastly reduced the number of breeds who hunt to kill, greyhounds, foxhounds and like breeds still in fact have this instinct highly developed. Many other breeds would hardly know what to do with the prey they had killed since they no longer suffer from hunger. Without this urge to spur them on, the kill is not vital.

In the wild state, dogs killed twice or three times a week and ate until they nearly burst, after which they were quite happy to laze between orgies. Nowadays, from an early age our dogs' gastric juices have been trained to flow at fixed times each day, and normally the desire to eat becomes apparent only at these times. It is true there are greedy dogs who will eat at all times of the day and night to the detriment of their figures and health, but these are the dogs that are easily trained by bribes.

The dogs that are the most difficult to bribe are the naughtiest dogs, because their minds are usually fixed on fighting another dog or running off into the distance, and I doubt if they think food will come from these escapades. The dogs that are most interested in food are the spoiled poodles and toy dogs whose adoring owners give them snacks at all times. "Just a leetle bitsie for Mitzie" has been known to do devastating things to Mitzie's mind and body, but here I blame the owner more than the dog.

Undoubtedly a young dog stealing food is a veterinary fault as well as a training fault, for many dog thieves commit this crime because they have worms and are always hungry. The food is not doing them as much good as it would without these parasites. However, the act of stealing is of course a training fault and has to be treated as such. The teaching of food refusal in obedience tests is a very useful lesson to most dogs because people often offer one's dog a tidbit; when the dog turned his head away and refused to take it, it taught the person not to repeat the offer. But it also had a disastrous effect on dogs sent to boarding kennels, because many refused to take food from the strange person who fed them and in one known case the dog nearly died. So now this test has been omitted from the obedience schedule.

It is quite certain that the mind of the dog controls its expectation of food, and one hardly needs a timepiece in the house because a dog's saliva will commence running at exactly the same time each day in expectation of a feed, and it is always best to feed at regular hours if you wish your dog to stop pestering you at all hours. The same thing applies to food as an aid to training. If a puppy knows it is going to get a tidbit if it comes when called, or retrieves a toy, it is naturally going to do what you bid if it is feeling hungry. But it also means that if you stop giving it tidbits it will reason that you are a fraud, and it will then be more difficult to train than ever. I therefore maintain that tidbits should not be used except in unusual cases when all other methods have failed.

This is especially important in the case of altered dogs, whose diet has to be rigidly controlled; old dogs, whose figures have already exceeded normal girth; and greedy dogs, who would never be satisfied with the small amounts given to them and would therefore get more cunning in the hope of getting more food. Nervous dogs wouldn't take the food or, if they did take it, would probably be sick almost immediately because the nerves have an adverse effect on digestion. Feeding a dog actually suffering from nervous exhaustion does more harm than good. That is why I never allow dogs to be fed during a day's training. I always tell the owners to wait an hour after training ceases and then give the dog one big meal and let it rest.

I am sure the most important thing about food in connection with the dog is to follow a properly balanced diet with sufficient vitamins and iron, etc.; for a dog to be intelligent it has to be sufficiently and adequately nourished. If a dog is lacking minerals it will eat rubbish and especially dung. How can one expect to train a dog to be a nice companion in the house if it forever rolls in nasty things, eats manure and has a depraved appetite? Again no mind reader can fathom the depths of a dog's mind and find the answer to an apparently depraved nature. Only common sense and knowledge of the dietetic needs of a dog learned from experience, books or your vet will help you.

Everyone knows that human beings either smoke or eat when worried; often an unstable dog will steal when it is upset or frightened. That is why dogs often steal when they are left alone in the house though they wouldn't dream of doing so when the owner is at home. The dog lacks security, and eating helps this feeling for some unknown reason; the only answer I can think of is that more calories are used up when a dog is worrying than when it is content.

19 · Indulgences

THIS IS A CHAPTER THAT needs much thought both from the point of view of the dog and that of the owner, I think more in the case of the latter. For is there one of us who at some-time or other in our lives cannot plead guilty to having indulged our dog? The mind of the dog tunes in very willingly to enjoy as many indulgences as it can persuade its owner to offer. Its brain is never slow to take advantage of every chink in the defense armor of its owner. The eyes of a dog, the expression of a dog, the warmly wagging tail of a dog and the gloriously cold damp nose of a dog were in my opinion all God-given for one purpose only—to make complete fools of us human beings.

I write reams about oversentimental dog owners spoiling their dogs yet know in my inner heart that not to do so takes supreme will power. For dogs are champions at heart stealing. Even the wickedest dog in my school who has severely bitten me makes me long to hug him close and force out his evil wickedness, and I love him. Dogs are not slow-witted. They know when to push the slightest advantage they gain over their owner. How many dogs do we know who have committed some sin and who have cleverly evaded punishment by bringing mistress something to play with and, with an innocent look of deep trust, waited for her to join in the game when at that very moment she should be stick in hand flaying the life out of him? But then that is the fascination of dogs.

Why do hundreds of us give up our holidays to stay with them, cry our eyes out when we lose them, defend them against all those horrid people who don't love them and on our deathbeds make provision for them in preference to our needy families? It is because there is something about a dog that gets you. Even if you own a problem dog imbued with all the evil the devil himself invented, you still know that, inside that dog, there is something very lovable—a dog that will never criticize you, a dog that doesn't care whether you are from the top or bottom drawer, a dog that doesn't care whether you are clever or stupid, beautiful or hideous, rich or poor. He is yours and you are his.

That is why a chapter on indulgences is difficult to write. For I in my own mind know that we can all read the dog's mind when he looks at the best chair, looks back to owner and again back to the chair, that it clearly means, "May I get up?" It takes a stony heart to refuse, although we know we should.

At my residential training school in the past I am sure I have shocked pupils by feeding my dogs at my meals. The dogs don't ask; they just lie down, waiting hopefully. My contention is that if my dogs don't annoy me and if I want to feed them, who is to say it is wrong? That is how I look upon all indulgences. If you like your dogs to sleep on your bed, putting up with the discomfort of not being able to turn over easily (especially if yours is a Great Dane) and having a snoring bed companion, risking the hairs and dirt on the blankets and sheets, well, that is your business. What is *my* business, as a trainer, is to see these things don't happen if you wish otherwise.

This is where a dog needs firm training, for a multitude of dogs get on their owner's bed and refuse to get off without a struggle and often bite the owner in the process. This is where a psychiatrist would easily be able to help, for he would know that, in the past, the dog got away with it and no probing of the mind is necessary to know the dog much prefers a lovely warm bed with a warm owner in it, possibly a hot bottle, and certainly an eiderdown to his own meager offering of a basket and a blanket.

There is no doubt at all in his mind that dogs love luxury. Bones instead of biscuits, beds instead of baskets, kisses instead of kicks, and if the owner doesn't want to bestow any of these luxuries on the dog, then the struggle to deny them must begin the moment the dog enters the house and must be carried on to its dying day.

My own dog, star of thirty-seven films, winner of sixty-seven obedience prizes, herself defeated rigid obedience at the ripe old age of ten and a half years. Never in her life had she been allowed to lie in front of the fire. The heat is not good for dogs. She was too big and took up too much room. Her digestion was not so good and Camay was not her only scent. Nevertheless, when we moved into a new house, she felt she would like a change and with audacious abandon lay full length in front of the fire.

At first we laughed. Then I said her name in a shocked voice. She smiled a sickly smile and the tip of her tail wagged, uncertainty backed by hope, and then, sensing my sympathy for her aging self, downed her head and feigned sleep. I pulled myself together and one word, "Sofa!," was enough to have her leap to her feet and climb onto her own extremely comfortable sofa. You see, her mind had picked up by telepathy that I didn't really mind her in front of the fire. In fact, I thought she looked rather beautiful with her brindled body outstretched. My own mind was weak. The dog knew at once. You cannot train a dog if you are weak or oversentimental. They know and you are lost.

Are indulgences wrong for dogs? I think, under certain circumstances, no. What does count is, can you give up indulging the dog without fights or disagreeable behavior the very moment you wish? If you can't, don't indulge your dog until you have trained it sufficiently well to be able to do what you wish at any time. The day the dog takes over, you are lost. I do think one indulgence is very wrong—that is, when you cannot leave your dog alone without its screaming or barking; should anything vital happen so that you could not stay with it, the neighbors would have to suffer appalling noise and you and the dog would be utterly miserable.

I think dogs should always go with their owners whenever and wherever possible. Yet some places you go to don't admit dogs. Occasionally you may have to go to a hospital or to a restaurant. The dog can't go with you; it must stay at home or in your car. If neither of these things has been taught by previous training and endless tests, you won't know what to do. This sort of situation is bad. All dogs should be taught to stay quietly at home for some hours; as long as their routine is not broken too violently and they have been fed and exercised, there should be no hardship in staying at home for a dog.

We know tidbits are bad for dogs; we know sleeping in owners' beds is inclined to overheat them and make them delicate; we know above all that giving a command and then not seeing that it is carried out is fatal to a happy relationship. We know that overindulgent owners have spoiled dogs that are a joy to none and a nuisance to all. I suggest we have a happy medium. Let's spoil our dogs sometimes; then we shall all be happy. The happiest people in this world are those that are forever giving and making others happy. I am sure our dogs are included in that.

20 · Rigid Obedience

THIS CHAPTER MAY SHOCK fanatic obedience fans. I have been one of them more by force of circumstance than by desire. When Juno, my Great Dane, was six months old I decided to take her up to the final test in obedience exercises and win in that class at shows—not because I am a lover of rigid show obedience but because, if one is to be a trainer of other people's dogs, one must be capable and experienced in matters relating to training. I had already trained dogs for police work, guard work and film work and as companions; now I would take on obedience tests as laid down by the kennel club. I wanted to find out what were the reactions of a much-beloved, highly intelligent dog to the set schedule.

These were my findings: dogs being tested will do anything in the world for an owner they love. They will retrieve ridiculous articles like candles in spite of their horrid taste. They will attempt to pick up pliers, pine cones and anything else deemed suitable for the test if the owner wishes it, even though their mouths were not designed to hold such articles. They will tolerate the dropping of chairs behind them, and strange people who try to force them to eat food their owner doesn't want them to eat. They will lie down on cold concrete or hot asphalt just because the owner wills it. They will ignore other dogs in the ring for minutes on end, not even scratching an itch, for fear of losing a point for their owner, to whom it seems to mean so much. They put up with having their ears pulled by admiring strangers after winning first prize, in the vain hope that soon they will be able to go home and be dogs, not automatons. Dogs being tested will suffer the torture of not having a beloved owner smile at them or even look at them in the course of an exercise, as though they had been sent to Siberia with only single words of command to break the silence. This and a lot more a dog will put up with. They will have learned the exercises just for the owner. They will rejoice with the owner when the exercises are over, hoping that each one is the last, and when the owner is tired of showing off what wonderful power he has over his dog, the dog will willingly return to being a nice, jolly companion doing lopsided sits and sniffing interesting scents.

The best working dogs are in my opinion highly strung, nervous dogs; the worst, placid ones who do obedience but wouldn't win prizes. To say dogs are happy doing competitive obedience, in unnatural conditions, for no possible reason except as a booster for his owner's ego, is self-deception. To carry on obedience until the dog is too old to move fast enough to obey, is downright cruelty. No one loves an obedient dog more than I do. For short spells I believe dogs like doing faultless sits if the owner is thrilled about it and smiles and praises with obvious enthusiasm. But what dog can possibly enjoy the tensed-up owner who strides martially around the ring, hand strapped over the chest, lips zipped, expression nil? No! Dogs don't like obedience carried out like that. To have freedom to carry out a difficult exercise with skill, encouragement and the combination of two minds as one, would be a joyous sight and occupation for dog and owner.

I retired Juno from the obedience ring in eleven months—five months too many as far as she was concerned. She and I knew it all; in fact, we knew so much that I shall never work a dog again in the obedience ring. I will train dogs for it if their owners wish, for I may be wrong, but as for inflicting these conditions again on one of my own dogs, I definitely won't.

How can the mind of a dog always be ready to perform so much concentrated obedience without tiring? The conditions of the ring where these gyrations are carried out are often appalling to a sensitive dog. Some dog may have puddled where our dog is to lie down and stay down for fifteen minutes. Does any self-respecting dog like to lie down in some place that normally he would go around? Does he find it difficult to hear audible commands when the public watching are making such a noise? Yet one distraction and a little bit of inattention and the dog has lost points. The owner is furious inside, even if to please the public he pats the dog as if it didn't matter.

I have yet to meet the person who could honestly say it doesn't matter. Can all this be happy for the dog? Can his mind really comprehend why straight sits, nose on owner's leg, etc. are so important? I think not. In fact, I think long spells of obedience the most tiring thing for a dog; there seems no logical end to it. For dogs a blue ribbon isn't a quarry hunted down or a successful track or a criminal apprehended. In fact, except to please the dog's owner, any obedience that needs barrack square performance must seem futile to an intelligent dog.

I believe all dogs should be trained in essential exercises. These are: heel on and off the lead; come when called; sit and stay there; down and stay there; drop on recall instantly; leave other dogs, livestock and things alone. This training should be commenced not later than three months old and should be ended as soon as the dog is competent. The owner should at all times convey to the dog by praise, speech and smiles that he has done well. By tone of voice, jerks on the choke chain or an occasional slap, if absolutely necessary, that he is a bad dog.

By the time these essential exercises can be carried out efficiently and happily on the part of the dog, kindly owners know they have done their duty to the dog and mankind. What more they do is done solely for business purposes or for the owner's pleasure and ego. I doubt if the dog is considered.

Give a firm jerk on the lead with the left hand.

THE HEEL

Immediately let go of lead with left hand.

THE SIT

Place left hand over dog's left hip.

Push dog to sit with second finger of left hand in soft "pocket" at top of dog's thigh.

Keep thumb toward your own leg. Do not put pressure on dog's back.

THE DOWN

With dog in sit position, lift one front leg and push opposite shoulder. Do not put pressure on dog's back.

Dog soon goes down on command.

THE RECALL

Tell dog to sit, stay.

Call dog by patting hands on thighs . . .

. . . hold arms out . . .

. . . and lift them to your chest.

Give the sit signal.

21 · Guarding

HOW DOES THE MIND of a dog work in the matter of protecting the household it belongs to and their property? I believe that under the age of twelve months it hardly reasons it out at all. People who phone me and tell me their five-month-old puppy is useless for guarding their house need to understand that if a puppy barked and guarded at that age, in all probability it would be savage and a pest when adult. The development of the mind in different breeds of dogs varies vastly. A Saint Bernard might not be fully developed at two years old, while a terrier may behave like a grown dog at twelve months. One cannot compare the development of breeds or individual dogs regarding their protective instinct or their desire to be a guard dog.

The upbringing of a dog counts for so much in these matters. Most puppies of up to say six months or over are, unless they have nervous temperaments, boisterous and friendly to all and that is how it should be. If they are put out into the yard for long periods to find their own amusement they will probably become scrappy and bark at everyone for a long time. The reason for this is that the early, developing mind of a dog doesn't know whom or what to guard. But when kept in the house with its owner the place to be guarded is quite plainly defined in the dog's brain. The yard, however, is a very different matter, especially in a built-up area with lots of people passing by.

At first the dog is quite good, only barking at people who enter the premises; then he finds to his delight that they pause when he barks, and he begins to feel superior and important. Thus his lack of respect toward mankind is established. Next he tries barking at people walking down the street, and at passing dogs, cars, bicycles, etc.; perhaps he even starts running up and down along the fence with his hackles up, showing all and sundry what a brave dog he is.

He gets bolder, and as a deliveryman enters the gate, he goes up to him barking. The deliveryman automatically raises in the air whatever he is carrying to get it out of the way of the dog, and the dog interprets that as a sign of weakness. His ego grows, his fierceness increases, and now people who enter the gate find quite a nasty dog barking at them, one who refuses to go to his owner when called or to stop barking when told. The people back out of the gate and shut it in his face. That act alone annoys the dog, and the result is, he bites the next deliveryman who comes in. That is how a nasty-tempered dog comes to take his first bite at a human being.

In the dog's mind he is not only keeping strangers away from his home, but he is showing his superiority over man. Unless he can be quickly broken of this habit he will get worse. The owner is powerless to make him stop barking because he has probably not been trained to come when called. Therefore he wins all around.

If, however, a dog is systematically trained to give warning of the approach of everyone to the house by barking when kept in the house, the owner can easily make him stop doing so by making him lie down with the command "Cease" followed by "Down." If he doesn't stop, a sharp jerk on the choke chain will do the trick. The dog recognizes authority and quickly learns that to bark in the first place receives praise, but not to stop barking when told earns him a reprimand.

If he is so stupid as not to understand, the only cure is a prolonged session in the "down" position, about ten minutes. There is nothing so subduing to the excitable dog as this, and most indiscriminate barking is due to excitement. That is why when the telephone goes or the doorbell rings, dogs become hysterical.

Many people are proud of the way a young puppy guards and boast about it to their friends, but they will be more than likely sorry if they don't check it when the puppy is still young. I think that from twelve to fourteen months is early enough for a puppy to show signs of aggression toward strangers, and even in this case on the command "Cease" and a further command "Talk," the dog should cease barking and be friendly to the stranger.

How, from a dog's point of view, is he to know who are your friends and who are intruders? Some dogs undoubtedly seem to sense this by instinct. Most judge people by their scent, and we suspect that fear in humans produces a strong scent perceptible to dogs. Therefore I think we can conclude that an intruder facing a dog feels fear and sends out this scent, but I also think that some people may simply not like dogs and also send out this scent, although they are welcome on the premises. And so it seems sensible to me to train dogs to give warning barks at the approach of foe and friend and to stop doing so when told.

Burglars have been known to be great dog lovers and have been welcomed by guard dogs, so I think it is difficult for a dog to know a burglar all by himself. Having trained your dog to bark, he should clearly understand his duty, and beyond that we needn't go.

Special guard dogs must receive specialized training for their work, and that training is not for the ordinary owner. It is very personal and rigid training to be undertaken only by experts and to be administered only by experienced handlers. It is never for the ordinary householder, for a guard dog is potentially dangerous and ordinary people couldn't manage one and don't live under suitable conditions for keeping one.

The dog should understand that his owner needs only a warning that someone is approaching. Biting is not called for. I am sure any beloved owner would get full protection by an adult dog if he had been trained from an early age to give warning.

If your dog shows no signs of being a natural guard, don't let him have the run of the yard; teach him in the house, by praise and encouragement, if he shows any signs whatsoever of a tendency to bark. If you have two dogs, the older one will teach the young one;

Both breed and upbringing count in whether or not a dog will be a good guard.

but two scrappy dogs in a yard can be a double menace and much more difficult to cure of menacing strangers.

When dogs go for me I feel no fear and grab them and give them a good shaking. I have been bitten, but not very often; and I certainly don't feel it until after I have carried out my job. The result is that the dog gets a wholesome respect for the human who shakes it and becomes wary of others, and very often one shaking makes it completely change its ideas about attacking. Unfortunately, we can't ask others to do likewise. All I can suggest is that the owner get expert help and advice if troubled with an overzealous guard dog.

Some dogs will never guard at all; their natures are so friendly that they love all the world. The only thing is to get another dog as well or have a direct line to the local police station.

22 · *Theft*

THIEVING IS A STRONG natural instinct in all dogs. From the earliest days in the nest he has had to fight for his existence. In the days of the wild pack his ancestors hunted and stole from those other animals not clever enough to guard their prey. The dog's mind is cunning in stealing and hiding for future use either food or some other article he fancies.

Much of the thieving by domestic dogs today is done purely out of boredom. I have never known a well-trained dog, whose day is fully mapped out for it, to steal. But the busy housewife, who has a dog purely for the children to play with, often gets a thief as a result of the dog's lack of deep affection for anyone in particular and of work to keep him from getting bored.

All dogs should have work to do, whether it be only tricks to learn from the children or obedience exercises or some real work like hunting, etc. Without this, their brains are wasted, their minds are pretty empty and their cunning increases. Watch how a thief dog sleeps almost with one eye open to deceive its owner into thinking it is fast asleep when what it is really waiting for is the opportunity to slip into the chickens' yard and steal their food, or into the owner's kitchen to see "what's cooking" and to take whatever has been carelessly left about. The obvious fear on the dog's part when caught makes us realize that dogs do know the difference between right and wrong if caught in the act or even if heading for where the act is to take place. Obviously, to know they are doing wrong, they must at some time or other have been scolded or punished for this selfsame act.

Dogs aren't born knowing what or what not to do; they only learn like children. Having once been punished, dogs remember, but like children, they hope they won't be caught in the act. Dogs can be so conscience-stricken that I have seen an innocent one creep and crawl away in shame when another dog has committed a crime, and the innocent dog has been punished in error.

I always remember that as small children we had a big and a little dog. The big one had her puppies in the barn and rushed out when a tramp came too near, bit him, and streaked back before the tramp knew which dog had bitten him; the tiny one just stood there and watched. The tramp swore black and blue it was the little dog that had done the deed, and if I had not seen the other one do it the little one would have been punished.

Sometimes dogs steal with a praiseworthy motive. Earlier in this book I mentioned Argus, my Alsatian, who with his mate made a nest for their family. When Andy, his mate, had her puppies down in that burrow, Argus, never having stolen before, went through a phase of thieving. One day I saw him steal some meat from the kitchen table and streak out to the orchard and drop it into the burrow and bark. I never scolded him, for I knew that in this case nature and the instinct to provide for his family were above all the training he had received.

I think, therefore, that owners should try to find the reason for a theft before correcting the dog. Sometimes worms produce a terrible hunger in dogs and a depraved appetite. When cured of these the dog no longer steals. Punish only when you are sure that you as owner have not neglected your dog.

23 · *The Mind of the Owner*

HAVING, I HOPE, in the earlier chapters of this book outlined the way a dog's mind works in a number of situations, I feel that no book of this sort would be complete without a little probing into the minds of a cross section of dog owners.

No one in particular comes to my mind as I write, just a mixture of dog owners and dog lovers I have met in the past thirty years of loving dogs. Some of them have thrilled me; some have shocked me. On meeting some I have been sorry for their dogs; with others I would almost like to change places with their dogs, or at least be reincarnated as their dog.

The thing that has always struck me forcibly is how awful it must be to be a dog. You don't choose the home you live in or the owner. If you want to leave an unhappy home, you run away or commit crimes for which you get punished. If you run away you are either taken back to the same home or given away to another home, which may prove just as horrid. If you are not claimed or do not find another home, your short life on this earth may be ended for you by a welfare society.

You can't argue with your owner except by refusing to carry out his commands or, in worse cases, biting the person you disagree with. You can't speak, so a psychiatrist can't help you. The vet only examines you and gives an opinion as to your state of health. A trainer may or may not understand you and for brief moments give you supreme happiness or dejected hopelessness. Yet with all the troubles in the world you are always ready to give unbounding love and affection to those to whom you belong, if only they will understand you. You can read the mind of your owner and all with whom you come in contact; yet your simplest wants are often misunderstood by humans.

You are always interested in things like smells, which human beings seem to totally disregard, and if a certain smell particularly interests you so that you don't even hear your owner calling, you will have a cross owner.

You are often left behind suddenly in a strange boarding kennel with people you may not know or like and a multitude of other dogs who are also bewildered because their owners seem to have abandoned them. You show how upset you were when they do eventually come and get you by an overpowering welcome; yet the same thing happens again and the owners seem to completely misunderstand your dread of being deserted. Weeks before they leave you, you have picked up by telepathy the unrest in the household as the time approaches for their departure, and you know you are to be left once more with strangers, with no assurance that you will ever see your owners again.

You are encouraged to defend your home; yet if you defend it too well and bite that nasty-looking man in a black hat who swaggers up the drive, you are punished for biting and probably shut up somewhere. How were you to know which people needed biting and which people just needed frightening?

Yes, I am afraid the life of a dog is a hard one.

What I as a trainer cannot understand about owners' minds is what they really wish us trainers to do or, better still, how they expect us to carry out our work without apparently correcting a dog or its owner.

As far as I can make out, if you correct their children, you are almost hated; if you correct their dogs, they can hardly bear it. Do they honestly hope that, having spoiled a dog for as long as five years, the trainer can alter all that without the willing cooperation of the owner? Many owners long to be cooperative, but their tender natures recoil at having a poor dumb animal treated firmly even though the dog obviously prefers the trainer to themselves and never shows the slightest sign of being frightened or hurt by the treatment it gets.

I suspect that what they would really like to see when they first arrive in school is that the treatment of the dog is exactly what they have always done at home but that now it will have an entirely different outcome, so that they won't have to change their methods too drastically.

I believe that a trainer has to change completely most dog owners' ideas on what a dog likes to make certain the future for that dog and its owners will be a happy one.

I have in only a very few cases found a lack of cooperation by owners after two or three sessions of training, after which they appreciate that they knew little about a dog's mind.

I always hope that people bringing their dog for training will do so in the same frame of mind as they bring their children to the dentist or doctor, realizing that to train a dog well and quickly needs 100 percent cooperation between dog owner and trainer. There may be a few bad trainers to whom training is only an exploitation of an owner's ego or their own business acumen, but most trainers are real dog lovers to whom training is a calling.

Few owners realize that the training of dogs, if done conscientiously, is quite a dangerous occupation and that if a trainer is bitten badly many times, he could suffer a loss of confidence in his ability, which could be fatal to his work. Therefore, the owner should want the dog to like the trainer and not be cross if it shows pleasure on being handled by the trainer. The owner should realize the association is only for a very short time and its sole object is to make owner and dog happy together. If this can be achieved with the dog supremely happy in learning its lessons, it is wonderful for the dog, although the owner naturally doesn't like sharing his or her dog's affection with a stranger.

Sometimes harsh measures have to be taken with dogs who are

out of control. At these times the mind of the owner should try not to send out waves of horror or to think, "I can't stand this; I shall take my dog home," for soon the stormy scene will become a placid one and the dog will have been taught for life that respect is necessary for true happiness.

Rushing from one training school to another only bewilders a dog, for every trainer has his own tried methods and is unlikely to be impressed or influenced by other ways that the owner might have been taught. Most trainers can tell if their pupils have been to another school, so the owner shouldn't try to deny it, for dog trainers long ago learned that absolute honesty in dealing with dogs is essential. If the owner is a bit of a "storyteller," the dog will not be the easiest to train.

The mind of the owner matters much more than the physical abilities; therefore, never give up the thought of training your dog because you are not 100 percent fit. You can be helped to achieve the true companionship of a suitable dog. Unsuitable breeds should not be acquired by physically handicapped or unfit owners. It is not fair to dog or owner.

Many trainers of dogs develop a marked telepathy with their pupils which also covers the owner's thoughts, so be careful what you are thinking in case the trainer can read your mind like a book.

And remember, if things get too bad, the owner can pay for a visit to a psychiatrist, but I strongly recommend that the dog stay at home. For the training of a dog by kind but firm methods is the best way to deal with any normal or problem dog. I believe the problems lie more with the owners than with the dogs. The daily living conditions of many people are hardly suitable for a dog.

After all, dogs were really meant to live natural lives whereby they probably ran at least twenty miles per day in pursuit of food. Their instincts were highly developed to gauge by scent alone the approach of danger, and their lives were fraught with the risk of sudden death.

Now most of that is passed. The sniffing of a lamp post by a male dog not inoculated against leptospirosis is far more likely to cause quick death than murder by another animal or human being. No longer can a dog wander off and fight to annex a wife for himself by sheer force of superior masculinity. He is expected to behave at all times like a gentleman and ignore the calls of nature. Do you wonder sometimes his mind gets a bit disturbed? He doesn't always fit into apartment life in a big city.

I think dogs on the whole are very accommodating creatures. They love human companionship and endure hours of boredom in the hope that a walk or a game will come their way. They endure beauty treatment that in the past no self-respecting dog would have endured. They have to eat what is given to them instead of pouncing on the nearest sheep and gorging their tummies. And cats mustn't be chased.

In return for all of this they get a warm, comfortable home, vitaminized food of the right quality to ensure that all their vital organs are nourished and sustained. They get as much exercise as the health and desire of their owner permit. They sometimes get unrestricted romps with interesting dogs, and if their owners are sensible, they learn their lessons like human children. Sometimes they get too little affection; often they get overwhelming affection, which has an effect exactly opposite to that which the owner thinks it will have. Occasionally unfortunate dogs get only hatred, misunderstanding and despair for a bedfellow.

The mind of a dog is really very simple to understand. All it wants is to have someone to love and respect, to be given a reasonable amount of fun, to be useful to its owner and to have a comfortable well-fed tummy. At certain times its mind is almost exclusively on sex; then it is not easily controlled by the owner. On the whole, the life of the dog and owner have to be in tune to get perfection out of the partnership. Both must respect each other's likes and dislikes, and a deep understanding must exist between them.

There are many misfits in the canine and human world, some that could never be put right. The putting of a dog to sleep when a problem exists that is often the owner's fault, has always seemed to me to be unfair, but I doubt if in a civilized world it will ever be possible to have it the other way around.

24 • Living with Mentally Unstable Dogs

UNDOUBTEDLY IF WE weren't such dog lovers people like me might be out of a job, for mentally unstable dogs abound these days. Some are born unstable, some are made unstable by their living conditions, but the result is the same: the dogs, instead of being a joy to their owners, are a worry, an expense, and often bring complete despair to an entire family, for few owners can believe the puppy that was so sweet at eight weeks old can be the vicious, nervous or cunning creature it is at eighteen months.

What I want to consider is that some people are determined to keep these dogs rather than admit defeat, or purely because their affection for them makes the idea of putting them to sleep when so young quite out of the question. So now I want to discuss ways and means of living reasonably peacefully with mentally unstable dogs.

Let's take the dog first that shrieks in cars. Is his owner never to go for a drive taking him along? If training has proved completely ineffective, what is the answer? I think it is quite simple. First, the owner must study her own driving methods. Is she a bad driver, jamming on the brakes, accelerating suddenly, turning corners on one wheel, cursing other motorists who don't comply with her wishes? Well, that is the sort of motorist that makes dogs scream in cars. Once I was driven at night to a film studio with Juno, my Great Dane. She had driven with me all her life and had slept most of the miles we covered. This drive was a nightmare. The driver was nervous and made me feel that my time was up at least ten times in twenty-two miles. The dog picked up my nerves, braced her feet against the car door at every corner or red light, panted and showed obvious distress. Had she been a young dog she might have barked or whined in fear. The car was too small to allow me to turn around and comfort her, and the result was that we were wrecks when we arrived at our destination. This one drive with a bad driver had been enough to make my dog frightened, after which if I inadvertently braked suddenly she lost confidence and showed distress. It took me some weeks to get her confidence back by driving steadily.

Doesn't this make one realize how easily a highly strung dog can get into such a state of nerves if the driver of the car it is in is erratic? Therefore the first thing I would do, if I had a dog that jumps about or shrieks or barks in a car, is to reassess my own standard of driving. Make an effort to drive with more thought for the nerves of the dog as well as for the safety of other road users.

In connection with this, it often occurs that the husband of the driver, or the wife, nags perpetually while being driven, or automatically jams down an imaginary footbrake. No one thinks either of these two things affects a dog, but they do. The mind of a dog is acutely tuned in to all brain reactions of its owners and a sense of anger or frustration on the part of a member of the family is quickly communicated to the dog.

Having examined your driving methods and found them perfect, the next thing to do is to think how the dog can be kept quiet while you and the family enjoy yourselves. Fighting him in the car will only bring forth anger from some member of the family unless they are all saints, and in any case, any disturbance while driving is dangerous in these days of heavy traffic, so I am not going to suggest that sort of cure. But what possible harm can there be in keeping at hand tranquilizers for the dog? I don't recommend these as an alternative to training, but, in this chapter, I am assuming that training has for some reason failed, probably owing to oversentimentality on the part of the owner. But even an oversentimental owner couldn't object to giving a dog a tranquilizer, or confining it to a portable cage.

I can instantly hear people saying, "But what happens if I only want to go on short journeys? The tranquilizer wouldn't have time to work and would last long after my journey is over." Well, the answer to that is, Why take the dog along with you? It is quite obviously no pleasure for you or the dog, so leave him at home, where presumably he is happy. Then I hear the words, "Oh, he shrieks at home when I leave him by himself, and my neighbors will sue me if I do that."

The only answer is to muzzle the dog if all training fails, or as a very last resort you can have his vocal cord surgically nicked. In about five years this scars over and the bark returns to normal, but in the meantime dog and owner relax, and one hopes that in that time the dog will have ceased to be a nuisance.

Contrary to what many people imagine, I have known some dogs so treated and have always found them normal, happy dogs with relaxed owners, and no one gets annoyed if the dog has to be left in an apartment alone. He is able to live his own excitable life without being a worry to his owners. The alternative was to put him to sleep. I think the dog would rather live.

But once again, this isn't the end to the dog owner's troubles. The dog, left alone without being able to annoy the neighbors, may once again come out top dog by digging up the floor, chewing the rugs, etc., so that it cannot be left alone with any degree of freedom, and the owner worries about what will happen next when she is out. Once again the answer is to make some place either in the house or yard dogproof. Either make a chain-link-fenced run around a doghouse or kennel so that the dog can be free without being able to escape, or make an enclosure under the stairs or in a closet, or have an indoor kennel and confine the dog there for short spells when you are in the house so that he is happy and not afraid of being left alone. Then, when the day comes that you are going

out for a couple of hours, you can send him to his kennel confident that he will be happy there. Once you are sure your dog can do no harm, your whole state of mind will change. You will give to that dog assurance that he previously lacked, and the dog will soon lose all his faults.

That is what often happens when dogs are given away as unmanageable. A new home and owner do wonders. The dog gets less nervy if the new owner understands how to manage him, and he at once becomes a happy dog. There is no doubt about it, many owners and dogs are complete misfits and the dogs will never be happy with this particular pairing. If only the owners had to pass some sort of test before being paired up with a dog, many unfortunate dogs would have better owners and many unlucky owners nicer dogs.

25·Dogs That Hate Men or Women

HATING MEN OR WOMEN is the most peculiar form of instability in dogs. They seem to hate sex more than form and can be sweet and happy with one sex and nervous or vicious with the other. What form of neurosis causes this we don't know. What can an owner do to make a dog with this nature livable? First, examine the owner's mind. Has she or he ever had a grudge against the opposite sex? Did an overpowering schoolteacher make the young boy's or girl's life a misery? Does she boast that she is a women's woman, or does she only get on with men? "I never get along with women, my dear" is almost certainly said by the type of owner that makes a dog hate women.

Alsatians are peculiar in this way and will hate men or women instinctively if thought transference comes from an owner with a similar dislike. So many women own Alsatians to show their superiority over their fellow men or women. They like big guard dogs, and the big guard dog thrives in this state of affairs and easily develops a dislike of the sex the owner wishes to dominate. Corgis do the same. I have particularly noted it in these two breeds, partly because they are highly intelligent breeds and telepathy is very marked and partly because the shepherding instinct is uppermost and they have a natural suspicion of strangers. Correct them firmly when young and one gets no further trouble. Accept their suspicious natures, and you will have dogs that hate men or women, usually women.

Now how do we live with such dogs? The world being what it is, we can't mix with only one sex. Even husbands or wives are a necessity, and it is often against the one or the other that the particular hate is centered. I think the solution is either to send the dog to be boarded or trained by a person of the sex it hates, or else get friends of that sex to feed it or take it for walks. If it shows any signs of being vicious, muzzle it and send it out for a long walk with the person it dislikes. Greet joyously that person when he or she returns and praise the dog. Make the person pat the dog and praise it before saying goodbye and, if possible, give it its food.

I know there aren't many good friends who will do this, but I think that if an advertisement was put in the local newspaper, some dog lover would respond. It might even help to employ a "dog sitter" of the hated sex when you go out so that when you are out, the only comfort the dog would get would be from the sex it dislikes. Only by being made to tolerate people will it respond. Obviously, if a female owner has been jilted and hates all men, her dog will naturally pick up this feeling when the owner is talking to a man.

In many cases, all these faults in dogs can be traced to some minor mental disturbance of the owner, although the owner may be unaware of it. I often ignore the dog and ask the owner searching questions to learn why the dog is unbalanced. When I find out what is wrong with the owner, the dog is automatically diagnosed. Dogs mirror their owners' inner thoughts more than their looks, as some people say. A dog mirrors your soul, for you can't deceive animals even though you may think you can.

In some cases when dogs have been cruelly treated by men or women, the resulting hate is purely and simply a natural fear. Then the only thing to do is train the dog firmly enough to make fear a thing of the past. Sympathy only makes things worse.

Take it to a club with the trainer of the hated sex. If the trainer is a real dog lover, get him or her to caress the dog and handle it as much as is possible in a training class. Once the dog has got confidence in a member of the hated sex you are halfway to curing it. The rest must come by constant mixing with people in crowded places where the dog hasn't time to distinguish men from women.

Undoubtedly this sex hatred is not a breeding fault as so many mentally unstable faults are, so it should be easily curable with expert help.

Never keep the dog away from the sex it hates; make it go among people all the time, especially if the dog hates children—another fault that comes from fear. Take the dog where children are coming out from school, to playing fields, etc.; daily doses of this will soon make familiarity breed respect. Make sure first though that subconsciously the owner doesn't also hate children. If this is the case, get someone who loves children to take the dog out and among them for you, someone who trusts the dog and won't automatically tighten the lead when children approach. If there is any risk that the dog will bite a child, muzzle it. I always fail to understand why people imagine muzzles are cruel; they are of the greatest help in training a dog, for when the dog is muzzled the owner's mind can be carefree. Time and time again I have met people who quake in their shoes and protest when I muzzle a dog; yet in a few minutes the dog pays no attention to the muzzle and plays happily in it. Most unstable dogs would be happier with a muzzle and a less worried owner.

26 · Abnormal Dogs

I CANNOT STRESS OFTEN ENOUGH that if you wish to keep a dog that is not normal, you must face up to living a slightly restricted existence. Although *you* may love a subnormal dog, other people must not be inconvenienced by it. If your dog pounces on little dogs for no other reason than wishing to see them helpless on the ground, it is useless to explain to the owner of the little dog that your dog won't really hurt it, for even being pounced on is quite enough to terrify a little dog even though it doesn't get bitten.

It is your duty to keep your dog on a lead and away from other people's dogs until such a time as it is cured of its bad habits. If it is unlikely ever to be cured, you must at all times see that it causes annoyance to no one you meet. I don't think there is anything that produces deeper rage in me than to have my well-behaved dog attacked by someone else's untrained and uncontrolled animal. Much as I love dogs I feel hatred at those times, more for the owner than the dog.

One person I know can exercise his dog only after midnight because it is so vicious that he cannot hold it on a lead when approaching another dog or a person. The dog goes completely berserk. I wonder whether an animal of this nature should be kept. Is it a dog's life to go for walks only when most animals naturally are asleep? I think not, but if the owner thinks it worthwhile, that's all there is to it.

This savage trait in dogs is terribly difficult to eliminate after the age of two. Up to that age there is a hope, but once a dog has got away with being savage for so long, the cure is usually wrought only by alteration and rigorous training over a long period. To have allowed a dog to be savage for two years means the owner lacks responsibility toward the dog and the human race and is therefore unlikely to cooperate with any of the above cures.

Alas! The mind of a dog of this age is all-masterful. He has obtained supremacy over mankind and the canine race. As stags fight to the end, so will dogs; and if the dog is a big breed, the necessary strength needed to correct him is often absent in owner or trainer. It is for this reason alone that I think the dog should be put away. For there may come a day when the owner is ill and someone less efficient is left to cope with the dog. Then an accident may occur, perhaps even causing the death of another much-beloved dog.

People often mix up vices with unbalanced minds. The two things should never be confused. A dog that eats its own excreta or the droppings of farm animals hasn't an unbalanced mind. No training is likely to eliminate it completely, for this is a nutritional fault or an infection by parasites. Given sufficient minerals, the dog will often become completely normal. If punished for these things, the dog loses faith in his owner, for he is only doing what nature urges him to do to find the minerals his body needs. Without training, a dog will cease this filthy habit when the mineral balance of its body is corrected.

Instinct is perhaps the greatest factor controlling the mind of a dog. Self-preservation, the urge to reproduce, the wish to follow a strong leader, the use of the senses to read the secrets of nature, are inborn in all dogs.

No one in his senses would punish a female dog for tearing the sofa to bits when she is immersed in that queer state the "pseudo-pregnancy" and apparently about to give birth to phantom puppies. To her it is all very real, and even if you scold her for digging, she will do it again when you are not there. If this does happen, the best thing to do is to keep her with you in these trying times. The condition lasts only about ten days, and usually, if she sleeps in your room, nesting doesn't occur. But if left on her own, especially at night, she will make frantic efforts to make a nest, with disastrous results to your furnishings. This is not a mental instability; it is a hormone upset and will right itself. To be forewarned is to be forearmed. Either put her someplace where she can do no damage, or keep her with you throughout her trying time. An indoor kennel is the best answer.

Only the owners of unbalanced dogs can really know where the line can be drawn between a dog that is sane and one that is mentally unsound. No one can make up the owner's mind as to what to do with the last kind. I, as a great dog lover, feel it is kinder to put them to sleep. There are so many nice dogs without vice or instability who need homes but have no hope of life because they are unwanted. Surely, when all training and veterinary help has been exhausted and there is no hope that the dog will ever live a reasonably normal existence, it is kinder to pet and owner to put the dog to sleep.

I believe that if you understand how the mind of a dog works, you will not come up against many faults that cannot be cured or made tolerable under certain conditions. I do not believe that a dog can be cured by a psychiatrist, but think some owners could be helped by one.

In the greater number of cases, a sensible attitude toward a dog's mind, not assuming it to be equal to that of a human being, is all that is necessary to ensure that he will be throughout his life "man's best friend," a joy to all and a nuisance to none.

The author and local pupil, Sally.

About the Author

Barbara Woodhouse, "the lady with the dogs," is already familiar to millions of Americans through her appearances on CBS' "60 Minutes" and the U.S. syndication of her enormously popular BBC television series, "Training Dogs the Woodhouse Way." Born in Dublin in 1910 and raised in Oxford, England, Barbara spent three years during the 1930s on a cattle ranch in Argentina where her extraordinary gift with animals enabled her to break in hundreds of wild horses. Married to Dr. Michael Woodhouse on her return to England, where they now live, Barbara has raised three children, run a farm, bred and broken horses, and trained 17,000 dogs on her famous weekend courses which teach perfect obedience to basic commands in only six and a half hours. Her Great Danes, Juno and Junia, made more than 100 film and TV appearances, and her own films, records, television series and books have earned her international popularity.